1100 ARCHITECT

WORK IN PROGRESS

1100 ARCHITECT

INTRODUCTION BY PILAR VILADAS
ESSAY BY PAT MORTON

THE MONACELLI PRESS

First published in the United States of America in 1997 by
The Monacelli Press, Inc.,
10 East 92nd Street, New York, New York 10128.

Library of Congress Cataloging-in-Publication Data
1100 Architect / introduction by Pilar Viladas ; essay by Pat Morton.
p.   cm.—(Work in progress)
Includes bibliographical references.
ISBN 1-885254-72-5
1. 1100 Architect (Firm). 2. Architecture, Modern—
20th century—United States—Themes, motives.
I. Title. II. Series: Work in Progress (New York, N.Y.)
NA737.A16M67   1998
720'.92'2—dc21   97-42047

Printed in Hong Kong

Principal photography by Michael Moran
Book and jacket design by Brendan Cotter and 1100 Architect

CONTENTS

ACKNOWLEDGMENTS

Our first acknowledgment is to our publisher, Gianfranco Monacelli, to whom we are grateful for the opportunity to pursue this publication, and for his support in the process of its compilation. We also recognize Suzanne Stephens for her vision of this book, and for introducing us to The Monacelli Press. The efforts and assistance of the entire staff at The Monacelli Press demand recognition, particularly Andrea Monfried for her support for the conception and structure of this book, and for her work on the text; Julia Joern for her unfailing enthusiasm for our work; and Steve Sears for his ready and valuable responses to matters of design. We owe a debt to Pilar Viladas for her introduction to this volume, her ongoing support, and her keen understanding of our work. Pat Morton, in the discernment and cogency of her essay, has energized our understanding of, and enthusiasm for, our practice. We are fortunate to have worked with Brendan Cotter on the design of this book. His experience, talent, and tireless effort have made an immeasurable contribution to our ideas for the book, and to its design. Stefanie Lew, our editor, advanced our literary efforts by giving clarity and concision to all layers of the text. At 1100, Molly Sullivan and Morgan Fleming contributed readily to the preparation of this material, and Ann Bobco and Bridget Brown lent advice on overall unity of the work. A special word of thanks is due Michael Moran, the photographer for most of the images in this volume, for his ongoing interest in, and clear representation of, our work.

The partnership that is 1100 Architect began as a loose collaboration with others, and grew into the practice we now conduct. Special recognition is due two individuals with whom we began our careers, and whose influence has been invaluable. Walter Chatham was a vital figure in bringing us together. From 1983 to 1986, while we worked with him, he showed vision and enthusiasm for the collaborative practice of architecture. Ines Elskop, our office partner from 1985 through 1990, brought principles of unity and grace to 1100 that exist to this day. She was an important contributor to all projects during this period. Consistent professional advice and support throughout our careers have come from Mitchell Koshers, Jack Van Horne, and recently, Jerome Wile. Finally, none of the work would have been completed without the extraordinary efforts of our staff of architects, associates, and assistants; we are especially indebted to their talent and untiring dedication. Similarly, our work would not be true without the assistance of colleagues in related fields, and the vast array of personnel in the construction industry with whom we have had the opportunity to work over the past fourteen years.

Commitment to our work began with education in the promise of architecture. We remember our mentors—architects and teachers—for setting us on the path of the work we now recognize as our own. Berge Aran, Günter Bock, Peter Cook, Philip Johnson, the late William Jordy, Luise King, the late Charles Moore, Elias Torres Tur, and Buzz Yudell each influenced one or both of us with their generous guidance, wisdom, and belief in our ability to practice architecture.

Lastly, this practice is only truly possible with the reinforcement and support of our families and close friends, who have seen us through all times. Our spouses, our parents, our children—you keep us connected with what it is to be human, and keep us honest in our lives and work. It is to you that we dedicate this book.

INTRODUCTION
Pilar Viladas

David Piscuskas and Juergen Riehm, the principals of 1100 Architect, consistently maintain that the only style of architecture they do is no style at all. Their stance is no disingenuous posturing, but rather an attempt to disassociate themselves from the design fashions that have come and gone since the firm was founded in 1983. Now that 1100 has built a sizable body of work, however, it is clear that that assessment doesn't quite do the work justice. Instead, Piscuskas and Riehm have developed their own brand of modernism, one that draws from the theory, the practice, and the style (or stylelessness) of the modern movement.

The firm's work is undoubtedly Modern—bearing the stamp of Wright, Mies, Kahn, and Aalto—and indeed it has managed to avoid the stylistic clichés of the last two decades. Any kind of overt historical reference is out of the question for 1100—they are, they say, more interested in architecture's embodiment of memory than in its expression of history—and their work is free from the strained attempts at "invention" that make so much contemporary design a chore to look at, much less to be in. Neither, however, does 1100 fit into the minimalist mode; while their work is restrained and disciplined, it is not reductive. Instead, it acknowledges the fact that human beings have to live and work in buildings, and that a work of architecture belongs to its owner, not to its designers. Nor can the work be tagged with the neomodernist label, with its connotations of fashion-world hipness and superficial likenesses to the International Style. 1100's architecture is far too earnest to be a backdrop for a photo shoot.

Instead, the architects have employed all the hallmarks of modern architecture—the lack of ornament, the open plan, the undisguised use of humble or rugged materials like steel and concrete—and placed them in the context of a more user-friendly brand of design for the turn of the next century. Reductive modernism having run its course—its limited vocabulary had made it off-limits to all but the most rigorous of architectural poets—1100's skillful use of light, proportion, and materials has helped modernism regain its relevance at a human scale. At a time when there is no dominant architectural dogma, and when permanence is often shunned in favor of the latest trend, this is no small feat.

It is a feat that was accomplished by relatively unheroic means, as so many good things are. 1100 simply follows the tenets of modern architecture, largely resisting the temptation to reinvent that which does not need reinventing, and paying close attention to the most basic aspects of design. Piscuskas and Riehm's work, while generally pared-down and free of ornament, has a consistent richness of texture, color, and light. They bring out the inherent beauty of the most rugged material by judicious use and elegant detailing—a notable example is the series of large-scale steel-and-glass doors that the firm has done for various clients. 1100's work recognizes the importance of the sensual—not just the intellectual—framework of architecture.

In plan, the work balances nicely between the openness they prefer and the sense of enclosure that many clients need in at least some parts of a house or office. 1100's plans are not arbitrary—you never wonder why you are standing in a room shaped like a bolt of lightning or a piece of pie—and even in an open space, ambiguity is refreshingly absent. This is another result of the architects' sophisticated use of proportion and light to differentiate between spaces—as in the Bleckner Studio and Residence, for instance, where the distinctions between living and work space are clear yet subtle, and where such differentiation does not preclude a unified whole.

When talking about 1100's work, it is difficult to overemphasize the importance of proportion and light. They are, for example, what make the TSE store on Madison Avenue such an impressive space, and they are what give the Reservoir House in Westchester County its relaxed elegance. In the best of the firm's projects, rooms simply become containers of light, rather than collections of surfaces and details. Not that the details fail to please—and the work wouldn't be as successful if it were not consistent on all levels—but it is that sense of light, packaged in the perfect box, that gives 1100's projects their particular poise and repose. When Piscuskas and Riehm talk about the importance of memory in architecture, they are also talking about the emotional power of light—without which, of course, architecture is invisible to us. Whether it is through a suavely modulated wall of windows, as in the Rifkin Residence, or an ingenious cluster of single-glass-block skylights, as in the Bleckner design, light is always the star, with walls, doors, cabinets, and hardware playing strong—but clearly supporting—roles.

If anything, 1100's work has in recent years become looser, a bit more relaxed, and more tolerant of ornament and pattern. But in maintaining its essential simplicity and rigor, loose never becomes slack. In an age that seems increasingly insensitive to—and intolerant of—nuance, 1100's work clearly demonstrates that it is possible to be disciplined without being dogmatic, and economical without being mean. It holds out the hope that modern architecture will not only lose its villainous reputation, but that in offering a humane alternative to the soullessness of the late International Style, the cynicism of postmodernism, and the solipsisms of deconstructivism, it might actually thrive.

David Piscuskas received a bachelor's degree in art from Brown University (1979), studied architecture at the Rhode Island School of Design, and received a master of architecture degree from the University of California, Los Angeles (1982).

Juergen Riehm received a diploma in architecture from the Fachhochschule Rheinland-Pfalz in Germany (1977) and studied architecture at the Städelschule (Academy of Fine Arts) in Frankfurt and the Architectural Association in London (1979–1982).

THE "DEATH" OF THE ARCHITECT

Pat Morton

To give writing its future, it is necessary to overthrow the myth: the birth of the reader must be at the cost of the death of the Author.

—Roland Barthes[1]

The death of the Author has been heralded and proclaimed by writers, scholars, critics, and literary theorists alike since Roland Barthes published his polemical essay of 1968. What of the Architect? In architecture culture, the Architect retains "his" status as unique creator and owner of the architectural work. The cult of the Architect seems to be the persistence of the Author myth to the degree that architecture might be considered the last stand of the Author. Or have we finally seen the death of this salesman?

11OO Architect has rubbed out the Architect, at least as "he" is traditionally conceived and understood, in favor of another architectural subject position. 11OO Architect is no Howard Roark. 11OO is multivoiced, plural, and heterogeneous, a creative locality occupied by myriad authors. Without denying its principals' agency and responsibility, 11OO Architect reconfigures the Architect and architectural production by supplanting the Architect's genius, individualism, and signature with bricolage, collaboration, and "stylelessness."

The Author is a modern figure, according to Barthes, the product of bourgeois capitalist ideology and its valorization of the individual as creator. The Author emerged from the Middle Ages as an outgrowth of "English empiricism, French rationalism, and the personal faith of the Reformation."[2] In this manifestation, the Author is the sole origin of the text, the creator of its singular meaning.

Similarly, the myth of the Architect characterizes "him" as another lone Author-Genius whose power resides in realizing "his" intentions in practice. The individualistic, heroic, and masculine model of the Architect finds its apogee in Ayn Rand's novel *The Fountainhead*. Her protagonist, Howard Roark, pursues his vision despite society's mediocrity and his clients' resistance. As one character describes him, Roark:

> doesn't work except on certain conditions . . . You must give him complete freedom. Tell him what you want and how much you want to spend, and leave the rest up to him. Let him design it and build it as he wishes. He won't work otherwise. Just tell him frankly that you know nothing about architecture and that you chose him because you felt he was the only one who could be trusted to do it right without advice or interference.[3]

According to the Howard Roark model, the Architect is someone who can and should bear no hindrance from "his" clients, particularly in architectural matters, because "he" holds a unique, pure vision.

In his essay, Barthes declares the Author dead as a result of a shift in modern writing and linguistics. Although still alive in histories of literature, biographies, interviews, and magazines, the Author has been eradicated by the efforts of writers from Mallarmé to the surrealists. Barthes asserts that the Author's removal transformed modern texts, resulting in the nascence of the reader. This is not to say that Barthes substitutes a singular reader for the Author; rather, he posits the birth of multiple readers, of many spaces of reception.

According to Barthes, the text itself contains no single meaning or potentially unified significance:

> We know now that a text is not a line of words releasing a single "theological" meaning (the "message" of the Author-God) but a multi-dimensional space in which a variety of writings, none of them original, blend and clash.[4]

Any text produces more than one meaning, and the discourse within which the text emerges bounds the meanings. Elizabeth Grosz's definition of "texts" as "the products of any kind of discursive practice," including verbal, scientific, visual, tactile, and performative texts, elucidates the nature of the architectural text.[5] The discourse of architecture consists of its texts—buildings, drawings, treatises, models, professional codes, etc.—and the practices that form them. These institutional practices are a network (like Barthes's dictionary) that determine and frame architectural production and its reception.

The text in architecture, like its counterpart in writing, is a "tissue of quotations" derived from countless sources, joining in "mutual relations of dialogue, parody, contestation,"[6] not the unique, original creation of a solitary Architect. The architectural text belongs to the already existing dictionary of quotations (crudely designated "precedents" or "sources" in historical terminology), which is infinitely redesigned and reread without being depleted. The meaning of the text is neither static nor fixed by the Architect's intentions, since it is the reader who produces its significance.

The reader of architecture is no particular subject, neither user nor client, but rather the place where the text's multiple references converge into a contingent focus.

> The reader is the space on which all the quotations that make up a writing are inscribed without any of them being lost; a text's unity lies not in its origin but in its destination.[7]

The reader creates the meaning of the text in a contingent moment of coherence, when the constellation of quotations provisionally aligns into unity. This destination is not personal, for the reader is without history, biography, or psychology, according to Barthes.

As an alternative, Michael Foucault, in his interrogation of the Author, identified an "author-function" that is "tied to the legal and institutional systems that circumscribe, determine, and articulate the realm of discourses."[8] The "author-function" is a "complex and variable function of discourse" rather than the generator of discourse.[9] This alternative presents a suggestive point from which to view the work of 1100 Architect.

What we have with 1100 is a complex, multivalent position more akin to the reader and the "author-function" than to the Author or Architect. The term 1100 Architect itself designates a space, the former offices of the firm, rather than the proper name of the Architect. The lucidity of two ones and two zeros manifests the firm's insistence on rigor and resolution. A shifting signifier for two principals (David Piscuskas and Juergen Riehm) and an unspecified number of associates, 1100 Architect is even ambiguous in its accounting. This is not a neutral position, or one that indicates an absence of decision-making responsibility. It is the refusal to endorse the usual cult status of the Architect's name. This claim might be made of any firm that uses an alias rather than the name(s) of its architect(s), except that the practice of 1100 performs a "writing" architecture, that is to say, a practice of "quotation" melded into "mutual relations of dialogue, parody, contestation."

> What is our style? There is none.
> —David Piscuskas, 1100 Architect[10]

This statement might be taken for hyperbole except for the radically diverse nature of 1100 Architect's work. What style label can be applied to a firm whose oeuvre includes an exercise in Miesian modernism (Robert Mapplethorpe Foundation), a vernacular stone weekend house (Reservoir House), and a poetically austere living space (Soho Loft)? The futility of trying to pin style tails on this donkey is illustrated by canvassing the canonical definitions of style. Heinrich Wölfflin defines a hierarchy of styles—

the individual style, the national style, and the period style; this hierarchy is the "expression of the temper of an age and a nation as well as expression of the individual temperament."[11] The claim to represent the "temper" of the postmodern age is ludicrous and a privilege that 1100 Architect resolutely refuses.

Christian Norberg-Schulz offers another definition. He elaborates a terminology of style as a development from the singular to the general:

> The style is a cultural object on a higher level than the single work. While the individual work has one determined physical manifestation, the style has an infinite number of such manifestations. While the individual work concretizes a particular situation, the style concretizes a collection of such situations.[12]

By this definition, 1100 Architect does not have "one" style, in the sense of a recognizable manner of expression that recurs in an "infinite" series of examples. The 1100 signature is not instantly identifiable through codified visual clues set in predetermined patterns.

What does characterize the work of 1100 Architect is a practice of bricolage and montage, rather than a fixed style. Bricolage is "work of an improvised technique, adapted to materials, to circumstances."[13] This is architecture that embraces new formal explorations and the investigation of solutions that emerge out of the conditions of production. The term *bricolage* thus implies the juxtaposition of heterogeneous materials and techniques that cohere into a circumstantial whole. A number of 1100's projects began as existing structures, such as the West Village Residence of 1989, an artist's studio and residence inserted into a warehouse [1]. The finished building contains original elements that were unveiled during construction (the vaults and a brick bearing wall), elements interjected from other contexts (the iron railing pieces), and entirely new components (the penthouse living space). The improvised qualities come out of incorporating the *objets trouvés* of the preexisting structure and accommodating unexpected situations. The integrity of the whole is achieved through the layering and combination of these assorted elements.

1

Meanwhile, montage is characterized by the production of "new wholes," in Piscuskas and Riehm's words, which distinguishes it from avant-garde collage technique. Montage, as Jean-Jacques Thomas notes, is a practice that strives to produce wholes: "At the level of principles, collage is characterized by the explicit and deliberate presentation of the heterogeneous nature of diverse components, while montage aims at the integration of diverse combinatory constituents and, as such, provides unity."[14]

Gregory Ulmer's definition of collage as "the transfer of materials from one context to another"[15] applies to 1100 Architect's method but is not adequate to its results. According to several theories, collage generates new meanings, new "possibilities of signification,"[16] through the juxtaposition of things taken from their contexts and "forced into jarring proximity."[17] The efficacy of such collage is predicated on the strength of the shock produced by the proximity of dissimilar things. However, collage's alienation effect is counter to the process of building a whole that emerges within 1100 Architect's projects.

The synthetic effects of montage and its application to certain architectural conditions pertain well to the work of 1100 Architect. Sergei Eisenstein defines montage as having a certain property: "that two film pieces of any kind, placed together, inevitably combine into a new concept, a new quality, arising out of that juxtaposition."[18] The contiguity of two otherwise unrelated entities produces a new unity that is more than the sum of the parts. The montaged components retain their integrity even while merging into the larger aggregate, *without* producing a shock effect.

The Greenwich Village Townhouse, for example, demonstrates the degree to which 1100 Architect can integrate fundamentally disparate elements into a unified—a montaged—whole [2]. In this project, 1100 Architect created a whole out of the definite personality of its inhabitants, the details found in the existing building, and a series of modernist interventions. Rather than slavishly imitating the owners' neo-harem style of decorating or devising a neutral container, 1100 provided elegant foils to the lavish fabrics, furniture, and artwork lodged in the house. Their insertions consist of terraces, windows, and doors that open the former apartment house to the city, in tableaus of roofs, the new backyard garden, and distant edifices. This treatment left intact those exceptional elements of the original house, such as the stair and door moldings, that warranted restoration, so that there is an intentional ambiguity between what is "new" and what is "old." The active exchange with the existing house and with the clients and their predilections results in a rich, seductive totality, an environment that envelops the occupant without suffocating them.

2

Again according to Eisenstein, the montage process of "aggregation" parallels memory's two-part operation: the assembling of an image and its imprinting on the memory. "A work of art, understood dynamically, is just this process of arranging images in the feelings and mind of the spectator."[19] It is this emphasis on the effect produced on the spectator that links Eisenstein's theory of montage with certain works by 1100 Architect. The cognitive operation required of the spectator in reconstructing the whole operates in Esprit de Corp, where the unity of the space is recognized only in experiencing it [3]. The showroom occupies two floors in an early-twentieth-century office building, a split section that had to be overcome in order to connect the large and small showroom spaces. On the lower floor, the offices are located behind the smaller showroom, along the exterior window wall, and form a type of space different from the entry area. While the reception area is a gracious, skylit expanse, the offices are intimate, interlinked cubes filled with horizontal light from the exterior windows.

The elements that simultaneously link and sequester the showroom spaces are components of the circulation and lighting: the graceful, sinuous stair and the elegant skylights/glass floors. The skylights, perceived from the lower level, are luminous fields of glass punctuated with slender, open, steel members that form a cross arch to the space's vaulted ceiling. From above, they disappear into the floor as patches of translucence integrated into the horizontal surface. In much the same manner, the stair changes in appearance as the spectator experiences it. It begins as a gentle curving single run and terminates in a baroque enclosure of Art Nouveau complexity, unseen from below. The spectator must retain a memory of the configuration of the two levels in order to link conceptually both them and the metamorphized forms of the stair and skylights. Continuity and unity are produced in the mind of the spectator as a complex, multilayered whole.

This unity is, however, a dynamic, kinetic one, simultaneously experienced in time and space. The fluid means of apprehension has affinities with Le Corbusier's *promenade architecturale*, a mobile perceptual mode, as well as with montage.[20] The observer (or reader) who physically walks through 1100 Architect's work constructs a constantly changing image of it, a sensual understanding that emerges out of the sensory appeal of that experience.

3

The extensive documentation of construction details in this volume demonstrates the close attention that 1100

Architect pays to architectural tectonics and the tactile aspects of building. The surfaces that come into contact with the body—handrails, door handles, moldings, stair treads, casework—are the objects of intensive scrutiny and exquisite, refined detailing. As Walter Benjamin wrote, architecture is a tactile art:

> Tactile appropriation is accomplished not so much by attention as by habit. As regards architecture, habit determines to a large extent even optical reception . . . For the tasks which face the human apparatus of perception . . . are measured gradually by habit, under the guidance of tactile appropriation.[21]

Although architecture culture is obsessed with the optical appearance of built form, particularly in photographs, the haptic or tactile experience is the primary one for the reader of architecture. The habitual perception of form includes the sense of touch, light, the rhythm formed by repeating elements, the color and feel of materials, and the resonance of sound, all qualities that play a strong role in 1100 Architect's work.

The sensual, tactile experience of architecture forms a central concern in the tectonics and expressive figures of 1100 Architect's stairs. As an element of movement and transition, the stair articulates the relationship of architecture to the moving observer and to his or her body. The stairs in projects such as Metro Pictures and the Greenwich Village Duplex form sculptural, vivid, corporeal presences in their respective spaces. More than mere vertical conveyors, these stairs enliven and activate environments that might be subdued, even verging on banal, without them. In other manifestations, such as in the Schwartz-Tuchscherer and HM/FM Houses, stairways efface themselves into the most minimal components: treads and supports that distill patterns of negative and positive, dark and light [4].

1100 Architect's working method, too, parallels the "author-function." Rather than the soliloquies and

monologues of the Author/Architect, 1100 adopts dialogue, conversation, give and take, the interchange and exchange of ideas between many interlocutors. Clients, designers, draftspeople, contractors, salespeople, laborers, critics, photographers: these are some of the actors occupied in the discourse of architecture. More complicated than simple "collaboration," the 1100 design process entails the solicitation of the client's desires and visions, the invention of program, an active absorption in the construction phases, and a continuous engagement with those inhabiting the built works, past the moment of punchlists and certificates of occupation. The term *dialogue* also informs 1100 Architect's conversation with the past, as seen in the HM/FM House [5]. Bricolage and montage are useful techniques for accommodating

4

the local Cape Cod vernacular within a refined formal investigation, physically and temporally melded into a new synthesis.

5

The Robert Mapplethorpe Foundation demonstrates the complexity of the dialogue since there was, at first, no one client and no clearly delineated program [6]. In the process of clarifying its task, 11OO identified the project's many clients in Robert Mapplethorpe's friends and associates and the foundation's supporters. The program that emerged is more of a living and entertaining space, dedicated to the community around Mapplethorpe and to the preservation of his work, than a conventional foundation office. The spare but inviting wall systems of wood and glass generate a flexible spatial system that can accommodate board meetings, solitary work, large parties, and archival tasks.

> Writing is the destruction of every voice, of every point of origin. Writing is [a] neutral, composite, oblique space . . .[22]

By creating a "writing" architecture of inclusivity, 11OO Architect engages the reality that there are myriad authors involved in the creation of an architectural work. Piscuskas and Riehm are not "ghost architects" who hide behind an alias in order to evade responsibility for their work or who credit mysterious, anonymous stratagems with producing their designs. They recognize that architecture is a social discipline, with multiple positions of creation, of which their own position as architects is only one. 11OO Architect lacks a "style" that can be sold to clients in the usual package of marketing tools; instead, the firm has established a coherent design process—out of bricolage, montage, and dialogue—that is as distinct as any signature. The collaboration of reading and writing creates the texts of architecture, the dialogue between the multitude of authors and readers who generate the work. The "death" of the Architect gives rise to the birth of the architect-reader, in the guise of 11OO Architect.

6

Notes

1. Roland Barthes, "The Death of the Author," *Image, Music, Text*, trans. Stephen Heath (New York: Hill and Wang, 1977), 148.

2. Barthes, "Death of the Author," 142–43.

3. Ayn Rand, *The Fountainhead* (New York: Bobbs Merrill, 1943), 317.

4. Barthes, "Death of the Author," 146.

5. Elizabeth Grosz, "Feminism After the Death of the Author," *Space, Time and Perversion: Essays on the Politics of Bodies* (New York and London: Routledge, 1995), 11.

6. Barthes, "Death of the Author," 146, 148.

7. Barthes, "Death of the Author," 148.

8. Michel Foucault, "What is an Author?," *Language, Counter-Memory, Practice: Selected Essays and Interviews*, trans. Donald F. Bouchard and Sherry Simon (Ithaca, N.Y.: Cornell University Press, 1997), 130.

9. Foucault, "What is an Author?," 138.

10. Quoted in Pilar Viladas, "Architecture: 1100 Architect: The New York Firm Lends Modernism a Human Touch," *Architectural Digest*, July 1994, 44.

11. Heinrich Wölfflin, *Principles of Art History: The Problems of the Development of Style in Later Art*, trans. M. D. Hottinger (New York: Dover Publications, 1950), 10.

12. Christian Norberg-Schulz, *Intentions in Architecture* (Cambridge, Mass.: MIT Press, 1965), 157–58.

13. *Le Petit Robert: Dictionnaire de la langue française* (Paris: Le Robert, 1990), 217 (translation by the author).

14. Jean-Jacques Thomas, "Collage/Space/Montage," in *Collage*, ed. Jeanine Parisier Plottel (New York: New York Literary Forum, 1983), 85.

15. Gregory Ulmer, "The Object of Post-Criticism," in *The Anti-Aesthetic: Essays on Postmodern Culture*, ed. Hal Foster (Port Townsend, Wash.: Bay Press, 1983), 84.

16. Marjorie Perloff, "The Invention of Collage," in Plottel, *Collage*, 10.

17. James Clifford, "On Ethnographic Surrealism," *The Predicament of Culture: Twentieth Century Ethnography, Literature and Art* (Cambridge, Mass.: Harvard University Press, 1988), 146.

18. Sergei Eisenstein, *The Film Sense*, trans., ed. Jay Leyda (1942; New York: Harcourt Brace Jovanovich, 1975), 4.

19. Eisenstein, *Film Sense*, 17.

20. Le Corbusier wrote that Arab architecture taught him a precious lesson: "It is appreciated by walking, on foot; it is in walking, in traveling, that one sees the development of the ordering of architecture." Le Corbusier, *Oeuvre Complète 1910–1929* (Zurich: Editions Girsberger, 1964), 24.

21. Walter Benjamin, "The Work of Art in the Age of Mechanical Reproduction," *Illuminations*, trans. Harry Zohn (New York: Schocken Books, 1969), 240.

22. Barthes, "Death of the Author," 148.

EXHIBITION OF SELECTED WORK
Frankfurt, Germany, 1986

Soon after we founded 1100, we were invited to exhibit our work. We began to reconsider the nature of architectural exhibitions and the traditional means of architectural presentation (diagrams, sketches, concept drawings, models). We then conceived an exhibition that would reconstruct the experience of the work even as it incorporated distorted versions of commonly understood forms of presentation.

The form of the work emerges out of absence. It is our desire to inhabit this absence by engaging, through praxis, a process of inquiry.

A courtyard adjacent to the gallery provided the main source of light for the work. Transparent images of the projects were mounted in mahogany-and-steel frames, which were inserted in a wall that increased in thickness toward one end. The frames were crafted with splayed sides in order to admit maximum light to the images.

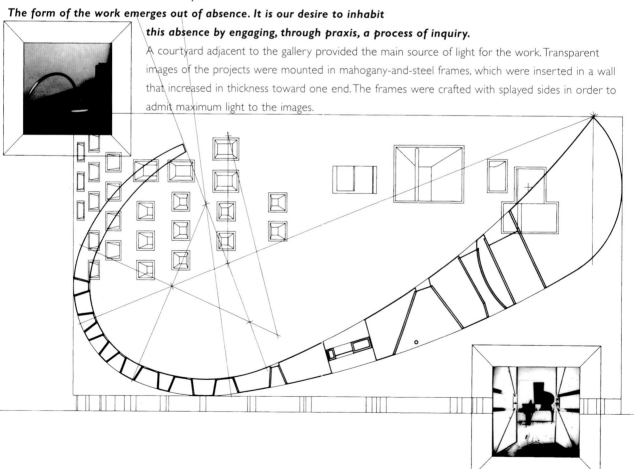

We maintain a candid expressi...

The exhibition is concerned with the use and connection of materials, and with an exploration of a lexicon of principles we believe are important to the making of architecture: shape, color, texture; light; permeability; and experimentation.

...terials as the prefiguration of 1100 architecture.

Small three-dimensional models of selected portions of the work were built in wood and set within the thickness of the wall. Panes of glass affixed into the opening of each frame represent an unconstructed void. Drawings—plan, elevation, section—were etched onto the glass to complete the description of each project. Furniture and objects were modeled, full scale, at the far end of the installation.

Total force required to bend 8-foot length of sheet metal (.16 gauge) into an arc = 4 adult males x average force of 175 pounds per foot x 3 (attempts)

ORLEANS HOUSE
Cape Cod, Massachusetts, 1986

For the form of this house, we looked at the saltbox; with its simple frame construction, it represents New England vernacular architecture. In its prototypical form, the saltbox is one large volume with a steeply pitched roof, few window openings of a minimum size as a protective measure against inclement weather, and inside, small, dimly lit rooms with low ceilings. Spare and free of ornamentation, the saltbox demands subtle treatment in its details, but is, in the end, rich in character.

Because the shape of the building communicates the regional idea of a house, it is reminiscent of colonial promise and an agrarian era of large families with many offspring to work the land. This house was built for the parents of five grown and independent young people, but a distortion of the typology is evident within. The spaces inside reflect the structure and transitions of family life, from the intimacy of an individual bedroom to the expanse of the shared living room.

The house is symbolic of a notion of shelter in its most basic form. It p

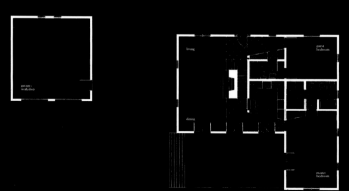

ses an inherent contradiction in that it has the capacity to contain, yet also to be unfilled.

Like a big barn emptied out, animals scattered, timber cross-ties cut away and replaced with thin steel rods, the house is dominated by unadorned openness.

31

HATCH HOUSE
New York, New York, 1986

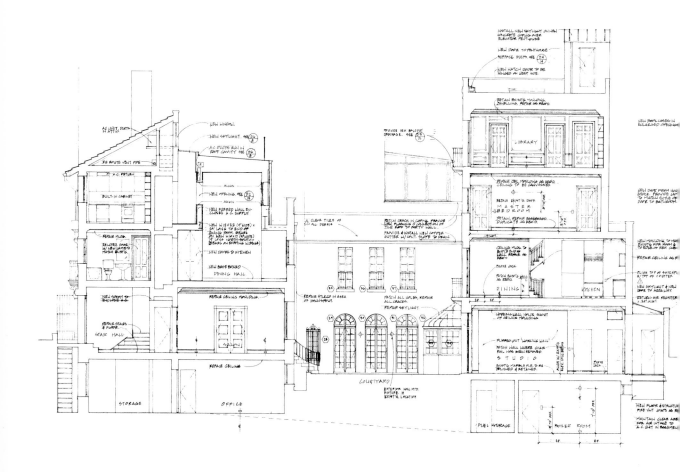

Layers of history are apparent in this project, the reconstruction of a landmark townhouse. Each of the previous owners—a Newport socialite (Cyril Hatch, the man who originally built the place), a theatrical impresario, an entrepreneurial ecdysiast, and a psychiatrist specializing in psychodramatic treatments—left an imprint on the building. Through time, and the personalized alterations of each occupant, the detail of the house became obscured, its central feature, an open courtyard, neglected, and its dignity eventually obliterated.

The work explores an architecture of preexistence through processes of extraction, interpretation, reinvention, and refinement.

The reconstruction work was limited by the covenants of historic preservation, which prohibited changes to the exterior. We concentrated our energies on establishing a new relationship between the exterior and the interior life of the building. The interior courtyard mediates between the public rooms, assigned to the front of the house in consideration of its proximity to the street and the community at large, and the private ones, at the rear of the site and protected by its depth.

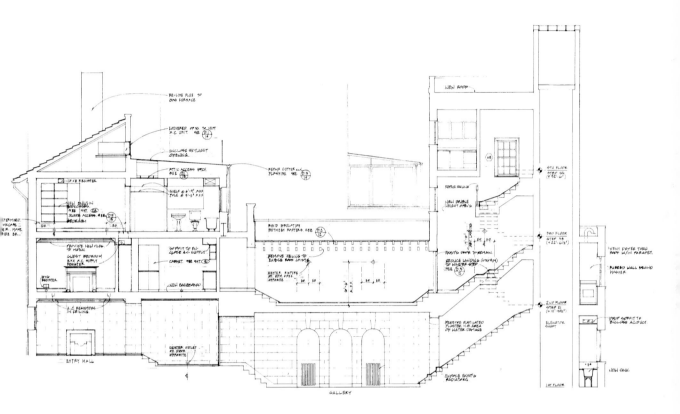

The building needed new services (and services it had never had) throughout. The dispersal of ductwork and the installation of air-conditioning equipment throughout a house nearly devoid of space for these purposes required ingenuity. We achieved a successful deployment of these essential components (even as we gave absolute precedence to discretion in the location of visible evidence of the system—grilles, registers, thermostats, etc.—and employed a healthy and strategically selective questioning of the established principles of air flow).

A relatively consistent ceiling height existed in the rooms of the original structure. To relieve the monotony, we created new spaces out of groups of two, three, or even more of the original rooms. The most radical change of this type occurs in the front half of the building, on the north side. Here, the house happened to be set back on the levels above the second story. We exploited this deviation to make a two-story room with the intimate scale of a small chapel. We followed this move with a reconstruction of the roof to create a light well adjacent to the upper level of the new space. Balancing the north-facing windows of the setback wall, the light well diffuses indirect daylight into the room from a new, long, slender skylight.

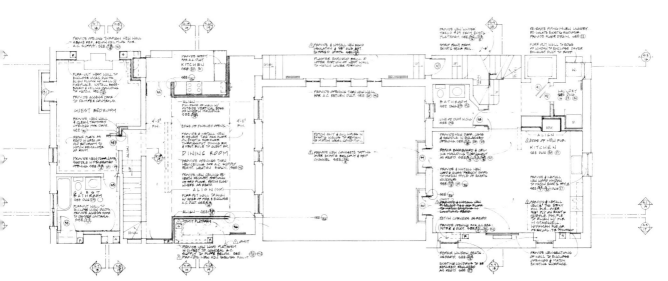

Occasionally we discovered, beneath many layers of paint and history, a material we knew and liked. In the entry vestibule and the passageway that parallels the courtyard, we found walls covered in smooth stucco, originally applied to simulate massive blocks of stone. Sometime later, a previous owner sought to conceal these rusticated walls with murals featuring scenes of Italian seacoasts. We preferred the original conceit and resurfaced the walls in stucco.

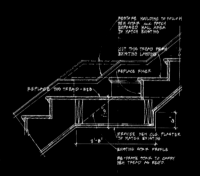

Motivated by the desire to create spaces of comfortable and human proportion, we rebuilt nearly every room in the house. A refined sensitivity to the living and working habits of the client now pervades the architecture.

Silence, in architecture, relies on a state of equilibrium; this equilibrium is achieved through selective simplification.

Among the unique features of the house is its back portion, which occupies the space reserved within most Manhattan residential blocks for open, garden space. As a result, this end of the house stands in towerlike isolation amid the neighbors' backyards, and light enters the rooms there from three different sides.

WEST VILLAGE RESIDENCE
New York, New York, 1989

Evident in the clients' collection of antique architectural parts was their affection for the past. The fragments, selectively disposed in new architecture, convey an abstract sense of history.

A facility for assemblage is a skill pertinent to our time. Assemblage thrives on a miscellany of elements, new acquisitions, personal memory, randomness, and precise details.

To give shape and human scale to the soaring entrance of the building, we employed pieces of an iron railing found by the owner. The railing became a material in its own right; extra pieces were used elsewhere in the house, establishing a continuity throughout the project.

CLIENT: There's the most extraordinary railing out here. You coul never build anything like it now, it would take years—if could be done at all. It's just lying in the grass of a salvage yar

40

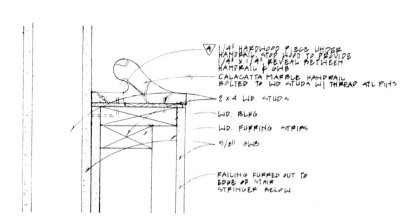

We wanted the handrails of the staircase to offer uncommon tactility. Molded to fit the fingers and palm of the hand, the new handrails are cast in tinted concrete with a fine texture. Warmer and more provocative than marble, our first idea, they establish an important dialogue with the new stucco and slate surfaces of the staircase.

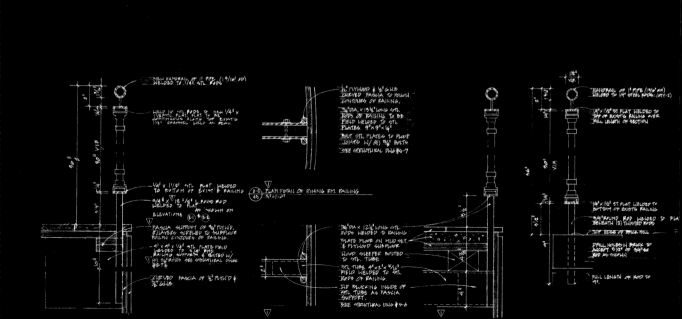

The original brick exterior wall of the second floor of the building (now an interior wall after later additions) had been ravaged over time. It required reconstruction + the owner had collected two dozen cast-iron pilasters + the space on one side of the wall, running the breadth of the building, would be one room with multiple entrances + we wished to remind ourselves of the building's original construction. The result is four arches with masonry spring blocks and cast-

Erected in 1912, the building first served as a steel shop, then as a supply house for recording components. Mid-century additions to the second story were supported by the installation of columns on the floor below, and led to the destruction of the original skylights. The result was a concentrated (and spatially disruptive) grove of upright members in a dark, but grand, interior. We removed these columns, replacing them with a more efficient structural system, and then installed new skylights. Now at the ground level there is a large, unobstructed, and abundantly daylighted workspace.

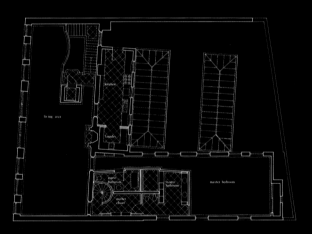

Although the previous additions had nettlesome impacts on the first level, on the second floor they were better disposed to contain the discrete functions of the kitchen and master suite with their abundant windows, good size, and sufficient privacy. The new materials that we used to surface these rooms adhere to the palette of new materials introduced in the entrance foyer: gray and green slate floors, hot-rolled steel frames, painted wood, and clear-finished mahogany doors.

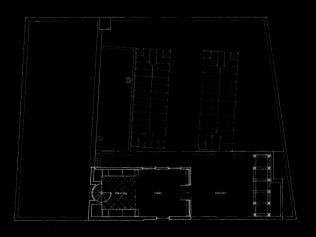

We designed and constructed a new third story to accommodate a study and dressing room that could not be worked into the floor below, and to anticipate additions in the future. Its method of construction derived from the rationale of the building on which it rests: brick walls on brick walls to the west and south; stucco walls on the concrete planks of the preexisting roof to the north and east.

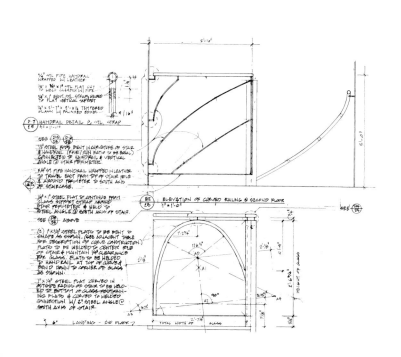

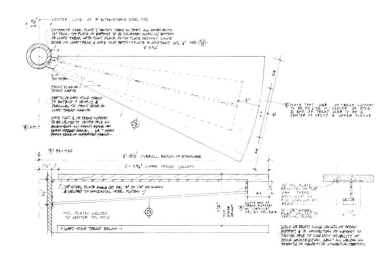

The owner expressed a fondness for glass block and spiral stairs. Combining the two in one place allowed us to breathe new life into each. While the new stair connects the master bathroom to the dressing room, we concluded that its primary function was to convey light.

The preeminence of light in our work inspires us to give it shape, then modulate it by differing degrees of translucence.

Surrounded by glass blocks, sandblasted in all but the top and bottom rows, the stair tower transfers diffused light to an otherwise dark interior bathroom. While it might have seemed inconsistent with this purpose to install a stair there, we designed it to be as open as possible, leaving the risers free and omitting the busy vertical rods of a balustrade (as in a conventional spiral stair) by attaching the railing to the wall or to the floor above, not to the stair.

NEW FESTIVAL THEATER
New York, New York, 1989 (project)

Inversion elicits the unexpected. A theater—a house— becomes the symbolic home for a disenfranchised community. The spectators—the guests —are really the inhabitants of this theatrical house.

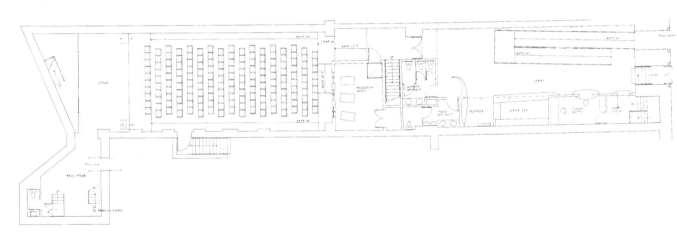

Home to the annual New Festival of Gay and Lesbian Film, this theater was conceived as the permanent location for a year-round program of cinematic and dramatic events. Its architecture is concerned with inclusion, not exclusion.

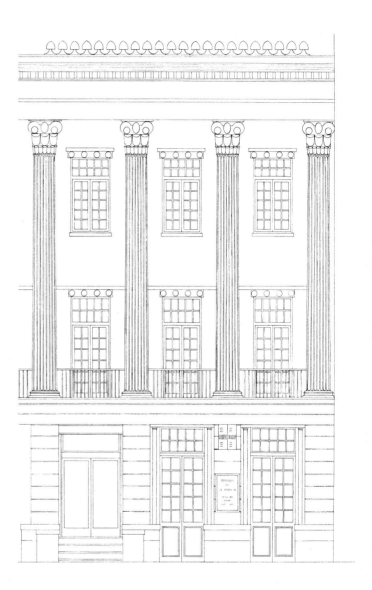

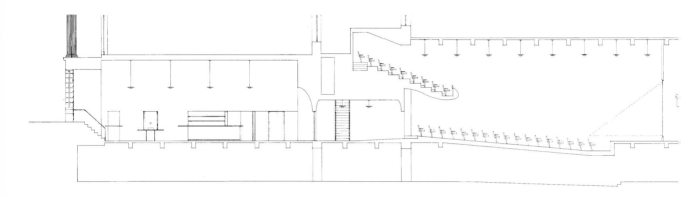

Parallels occur throughout the project, producing equivalences between plan and section, proportion and program, performer and spectator.

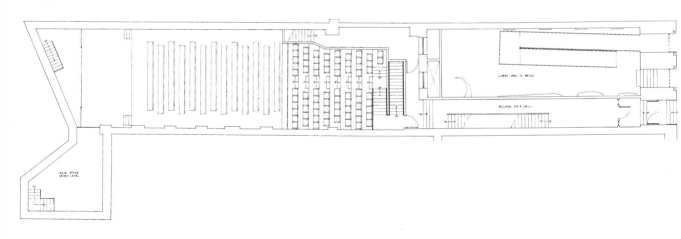

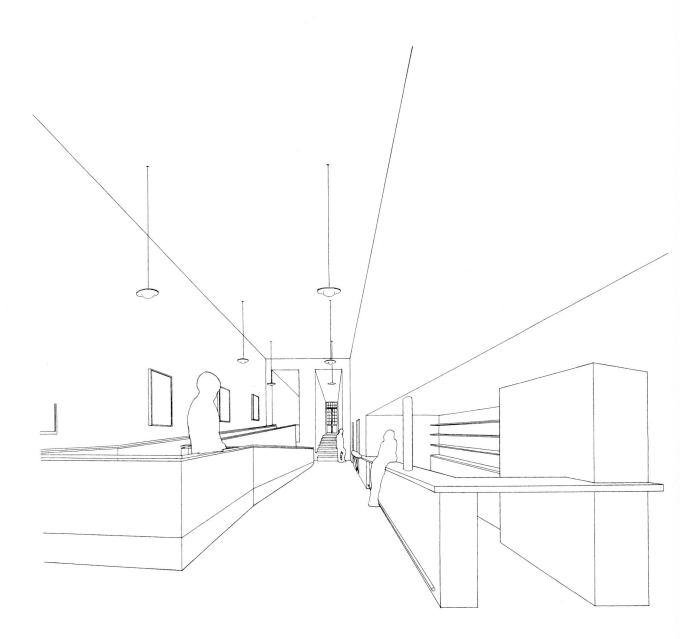

At the center of the scheme is the lobby, a space at once optimistic and elegant, for both arrival and congregation. For the community, as well as for the mission of the festival, the lobby is both the real and the metaphoric center of the theater.

An inclined path—a theatrical promenade—leads from the street to the lobby. The intersection of this path with the lobby is the nexus of the design. In the other half of the project, the demands of the program could not be accommodated without alterations to the existing theater. We proposed a shallow rake in the floor normative to a cinema. A modest stage ensured unobstructed sight lines for theatrical performances.

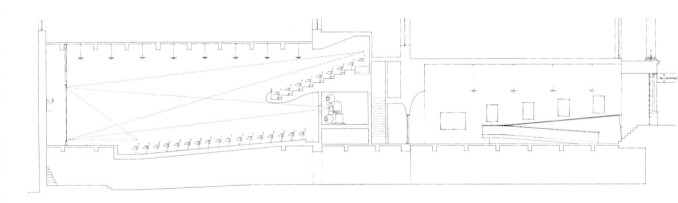

The practical functions of the lobby—coat storage, ticket window, coffee bar, and to a lesser extent, the bathrooms—are tucked beneath the seven-foot clearance at the south side of the lobby. The two-story area of the lobby is given over to ramp access and free space. At first glance the free area of the lobby appears small, overrun by the required size of the ramp. However, its size is in proportion to the number of persons occupying the space, and proportionately equal to other lobbies of identical function in nearby cinemas. By extension, it may be observed that if a wheelchair lift were located in the northeast corner of the space to convey disabled patrons to the lobby, the lobby would be too open given its new height (approximately nineteen feet). Conversely, the dynamic gesture of the ramp sets well in a space of the scale and proportion that result when the parlor floor is removed. The area that is not occupied by the ramp has been designed to facilitate the movement of patrons through the space, while at the same time inviting them to pause before and after a show. The lobby may be simply appointed, with showcases along the north wall as one enters, and eight milk-glass lamps hanging in a regular pattern through the space and enforcing the feeling of the lobby as a room, and not simply as an area that one rushes through on the way to the theater. Illumination of tasks related to the coffee bar and ticket window, and illumination of the showcases, will allow additional accent light to embellish the room. Elaborately finished surfaces should not be essential to the space, since most of the drama is gained from the new double-height proportion of the space, and the ramped entry sequence.

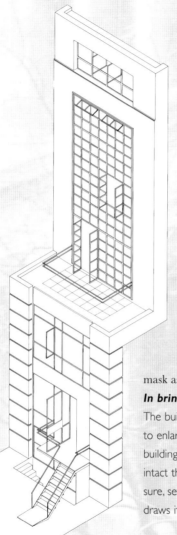

UPPER EAST SIDE TOWNHOUSE
New York, New York, 1989 (project)

We saw the two exterior walls of this townhouse as two vastly different masks. On the street, the facade was somber; landmark district regulations prevented us from altering it. On the garden, we envisioned a second, radically different, more open mask as a single plane, shifted at the third floor to produce a terrace.

In bringing the work to light we are interested in bringing light to the wa

The building was to accommodate a family by increasing its floor area, but to enlarge the structure by 30 percent was, ultimately, to create a new building. We increased the back half of the building by one story, leaving intact the five-story structure of the front half. The southern (back) exposure, set within the regulated limit line of buildable area, captures light and draws it into the narrow confines of the site.

Focus on the entrance of light—perhaps through an extended lens—and the spectrum of its movement through space.

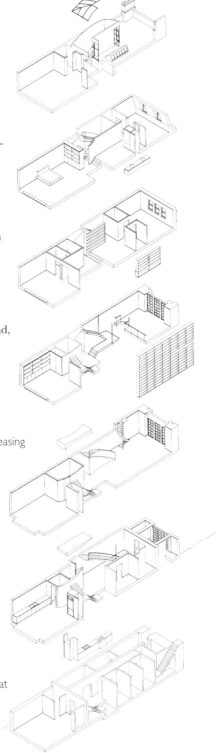

Just as the facades were developed with two readings, the plan demanded two separate but interrelated approaches. The first strategy was a horizontal one, concerned with the relationship of the length of the building to its width, and with the sequence of circulation from the dark front to the brightly lit back of the house. The second approach was metameric. Half floors, subsets of each story, were stacked and selectively connected like vertebrae, producing rooms of variegated section. In the end, the scheme acquired a tartan quality with its multiple horizontal and vertical crossings, aptly symbolic of the dualities that permeated its program and site.

The design of the house, from the necessity of increasing its size to the strategy for admitting light to the building, answered to an extensive domestic program. Service quarters were located in the basement, with daylight and air admitted through clerestory windows in the garden. The kitchen is located atop this area, directly astride the garden at the rear, some fifty feet from the entry. There, the vestibule opens to a grand staircase connecting it with the two-story library, salon, and dining room of the piano nobile. The third level, one flight up, includes two studies ancillary to the grand room of books, one that communicates with the garden terrace at the rear. Sequential levels of children's bedrooms and a bilevel master suite and studio complete the disposition of the program.

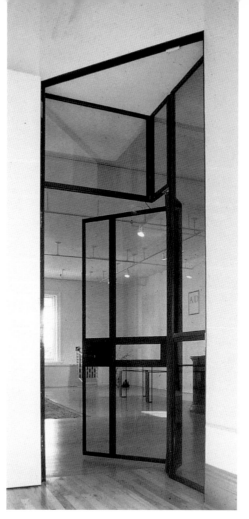

A/D GALLERY
New York, New York, 1989

A gallery owner approached us with a request to design the front door to her exhibition space. The existing door was wedged into a chamfered corner, and looked like an afterthought, not an entrance. However, the bizarre premise of a door in a corner was too humorous to ignore, and so we made the door a corner.

In considering the conflation of architecture and furniture, we observe an essence of duality: variant readings are brought forth by acuity, not attenuation.

By opening the corner, we brought light into the gallery from an interior court and redirected the path of movement through the gallery in relation to its point of entry. This not only effects a flow of natural light, but also affects the act of entering by bringing focus to the large volume of the gallery space. A sidelight in the glazed, steel-framed composition draws attention to the principal exhibition wall, and hints at the works on display beyond.

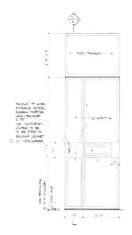

The A/D Gallery commissions artists to design individual works of functional utility. The works are produced in limited editions and sold through the gallery.

A steel-plated panel satisfies security and fire-resistance requirements. When closed, it reinstates the original location of the door.

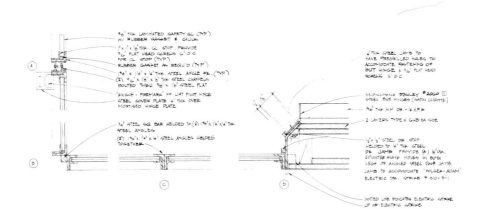

We see the work as an exposition—of conditions that precede our engagement, of light for a dark place, of the apotheosized rendition of components and materials, of the architect, the designer, as artist.

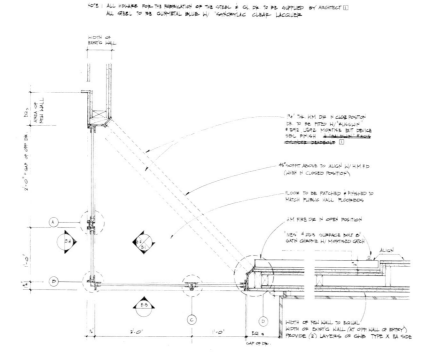

BLECKNER STUDIO
AND RESIDENCE
New York, New York, 1990

The work aspires to raise the consciousness of sensory perception.

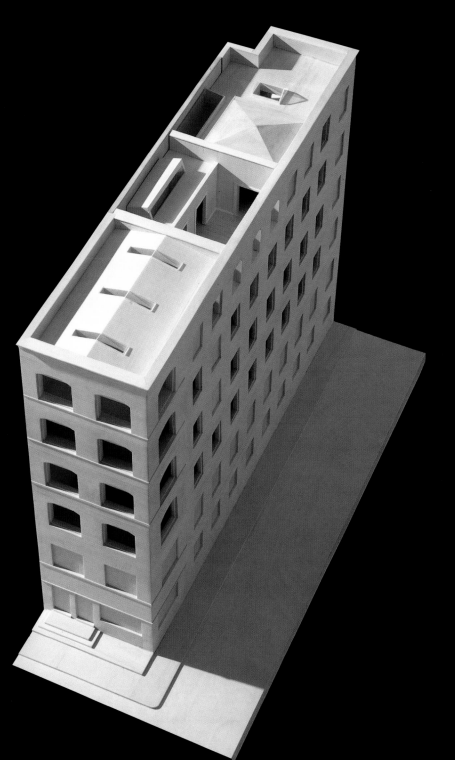

A window ledge, 120 linear feet of Douglas fir, perforated with $3/4$-inch holes at $1 1/2$-inch centers to permit heat convection.

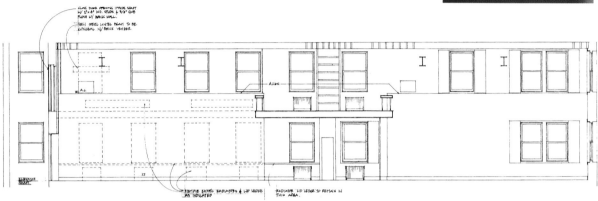

In a six-story loft building in lower Manhattan, the residue of previous tenants (most notably, the Mudd Club) left a history that clashed with the owner's vision. He desired a place where he could live and work comfortably and productively, a place defined by elegance and tranquility. To effect this we completely changed the nature and feeling of the building, and in the process eradicated nearly all traces of its former occupants.

We exploit structural change, regarding it as fundamental to the process of redefinition.

Our work on the first and second floors consisted primarily of routine rehabilitation to the infrastructure of the building. Higher up, most of the fourth floor was cut away to create a painting studio comprised of two double-height volumes on the third level, joined by a bridge (actually a remnant of the fourth floor). To accomplish this transformation, steel carriage I-beams were inserted into the brick exterior wall and run perpendicular to the longitudinal wood timbers that support the floor joists.

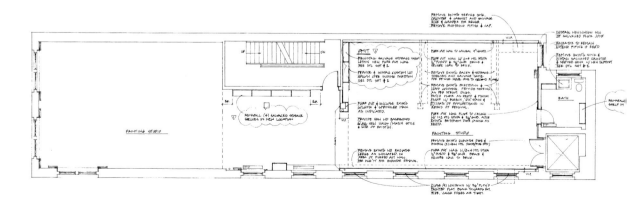

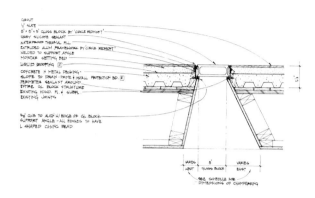

An architecture of optimism is sparked by the promise of light ascendant. It is stimulated by a glance of

Zoning restrictions dictated that our work be confined within the building volume. In limitations lie creative opportunities; accordingly the greatest structural transformation in the building occurred on the top floor and the roof. We conceived an outdoor terrace/garden as a void around which are disposed a series of discrete spaces. Glass blocks are interspersed with the paving stones of the terrace; these little skylights bathe the kitchen and dining area below in a muted glow of natural light.

ss a surface, and nurtured in the softness, the ease, of lambency.

On the fifth floor, which became the lower level of the duplex residence, we combined the rawness of the extant wood columns and beams with layers of new surfaces: a floor of tinted, ground concrete; birch veneer plywood in a new kitchen; a mixture of cement and plaster on the walls; and at the windows, an uninterrupted ledge constructed out of joists salvaged during the removal of the roof.

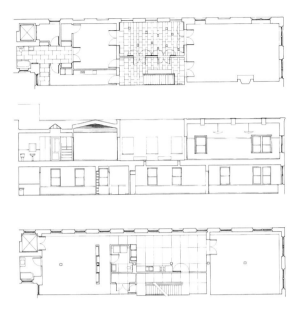

The outdoor terrace is the central element of the plan and separates the public and private rooms of the residence. It captures light within its well and diffuses it to the rooms both adjacent and below. This court is but the largest of the many light-conveying penetrations we designed in the building. As a result of our desire to fill the rooms with light, little of the original roof remained. It was removed in favor of distinct roofs for each of the rooms on the top floor.

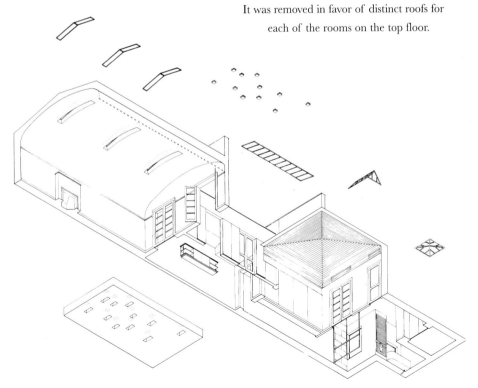

The top floor is the most refined part of the building, and was designed with a fundamental concern for well-proportioned rooms and the character of the transitions between them. These transitions are spaces too, rewarded for their utility by a suffusion of light. Except for the doors to the terrace, the bedroom lacks a window to the exterior. Its quality of light is balanced by the passage, through translucent glass in a transom and casement doors, of abundant daylight from the adjacent closet.

initial interaction between a person and a space is defined by proportion. The sentience we seek suggests a silent continuance of moment whose activation by light connects a person and a space in a way unlimited by material boundaries.

THE ROBERT MAPPLETHORPE FOUNDATION
New York, New York, 1990

This project creates a place of memory, where the life and work of one artist is retained and sustained. Memory, unlike architecture, is not fixed; it is a fluid phenomenon, influenced by the present as well as the past.

The architecture proposes a continuum in the transition from presence to absence, and in the coexistence of grace and controversy, passage and stillness, without bias or sentiment.

Essentially, the plan describes one coherent space divided only by juxtapositions of different materials. Inserted between the surfaces of these materials is the program: individual offices, archival maintenance, conference room, and living area.

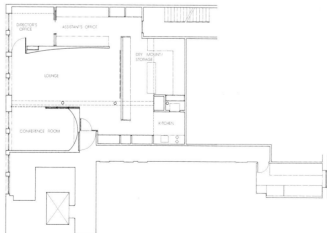

The Robert Mapplethorpe Foundation houses the archives of Robert Mapplethorpe's photography and administers the display, publication, and sale of his work. All proceeds of the foundation support research dedicated to the cure of AIDS.

1100: The conference area, almost a room, partially defined by a wall of steel, wood, and glass . . .

RMF: A conference room that can be closed, where we are able to have a private conversation . . .

1100: How about two walls, each the same? We can slide one in front of the other to close the room, but you could also enter or leave through a swinging door in the fixed wall . . .

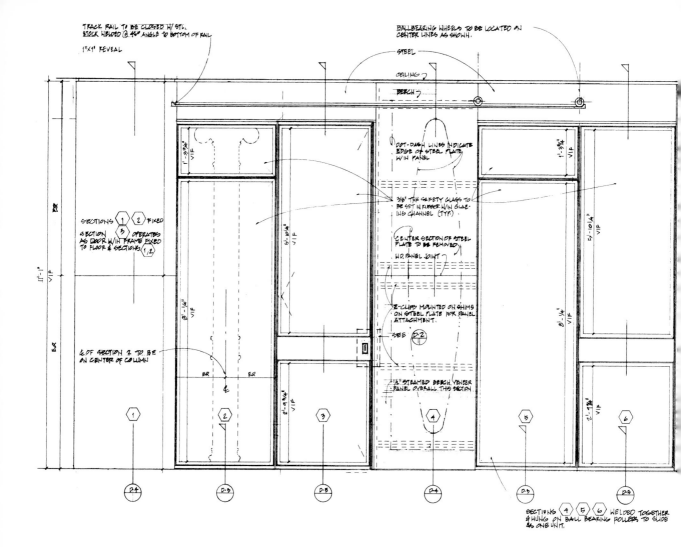

TRACK RAIL TO BE CLOSED W/ STL.
STOCK WELDED @ 45° ANGLE TO BOTTOM OF RAIL

1"X1" REVEAL

BALLBEARING WHEELS TO BE LOCATED ON
CENTER LINES AS SHOWN.

STEEL

CEILING

BENCH

DOT-DASH LINES INDICATE
EDGE OF STEEL PLATE
W/IN PANEL

3/8" THK SAFETY GLASS TO
BE SET IN RUBBER W/IN GLAZ-
ING CHANNEL (TYP.)

CENTER SECTION OF STEEL
PLATE TO BE REMOVED

W.D. PANEL JOINT

Z-CLIPS MOUNTED ON SHIMS
ON STEEL PLATE FOR PANEL
ATTACHMENT.

SEE ⟨2-2⟩

3/4" STEAMED BEECH VENEER
PANEL OVERALL THIS SECTION

SECTIONS ①②FIXED

SECTION ③ OPERATES
AS DOOR W/IN FRAME FIXED
TO FLOOR & SECTIONS ①,②

₵ OF SECTION 2 TO BE
ON CENTER OF COLUMN

SECTIONS ⟨4⟩⟨5⟩⟨6⟩ WELDED TOGETHER
& HUNG ON BALL BEARING ROLLERS TO SLIDE
AS ONE UNIT.

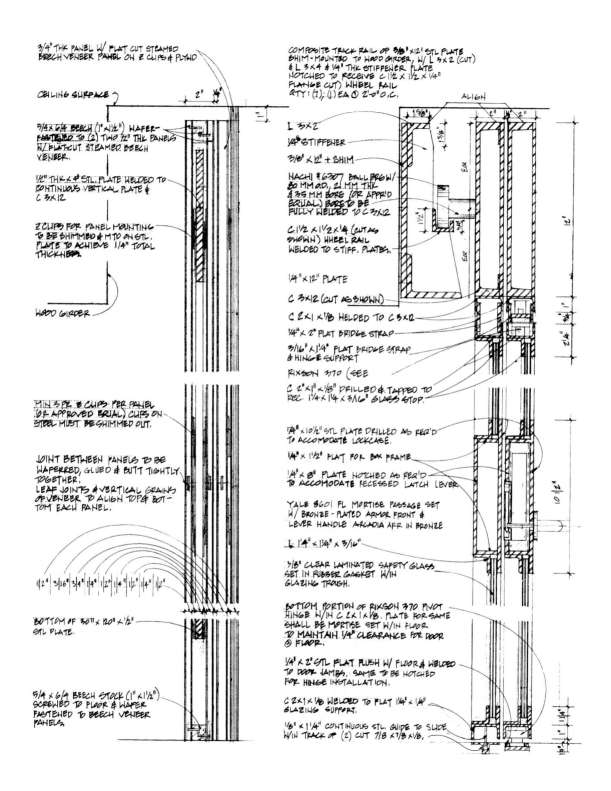

3/4" THK PANEL W/ FLAT CUT STEAMED
BEECH VENEER PANEL ON Z CLIPS & PLYWD

CEILING SURFACE

5/4 x 6/4 BEECH (1" x 1½") WAFER-
FASTENED TO (2) TWO ½" THK PANELS
W/ FLATCUT STEAMED BEECH
VENEER.

½" THK x 4 STL. PLATE WELDED TO
CONTINUOUS VERTICAL PLATE &
C 3x12

Z CLIPS FOR PANEL MOUNTING
TO BE SHIMMED & MTD ON STL.
PLATE TO ACHIEVE 1/4" TOTAL
THICKNESS.

WOOD GIRDER

MIN 3 PC. Z CLIPS PER PANEL
(OR APPROVED EQUAL) CLIPS ON
STEEL MUST BE SHIMMED OUT.

JOINT BETWEEN PANELS TO BE
WAFERED, GLUED & BUTT TIGHTLY
TOGETHER.
LEAF JOINTS & VERTICAL GRAINS
OF VENEER TO ALIGN TOP & BOT-
TOM EACH PANEL.

1½" 3/16" 3/4" ¼" 2" ¼" ½" ¼" ½"

BOTTOM OF 30" x 120" x ½"
STL PLATE.

5/4 x 6/4 BEECH STOCK (1" x 1½")
SCREWED TO FLOOR & WAFER
FASTENED TO BEECH VENEER
PANELS.

COMPOSITE TRACK RAIL OF 3/8" x 12" STL PLATE
SHIM-MOUNTED TO WOOD GIRDER, W/ L 3 x 2 (CUT)
& L 3 x 4 & 1/4" THK STIFFENER PLATE
NOTCHED TO RECEIVE C 1½ x 1½ x 1/4"
(FLANGE CUT) WHEEL RAIL
QTY: (7); (1) EA @ 2'-0" O.C.

ALIGN

L 3 x 2

1/4" STIFFENER

3/8" x 12" + SHIM

NACHI #6307 BALL BRG W/
80 MM O.D., 21 MM THK
& 35 MM BORE (OR APPR'D
EQUAL) BORED TO BE
FULLY WELDED TO C 3 x 12

C 1½ x 1½ x 1/4 (CUT AS
SHOWN) WHEEL RAIL
WELDED TO STIFF. PLATES.

1/4" x 12" PLATE

C 3 x 12 (CUT AS SHOWN)

C 2 x 1 x 1/8 WELDED TO C 3 x 12

1/4" x 2" FLAT BRIDGE STRAP

3/16" x 1 1/4" FLAT BRIDGE STRAP
& HINGE SUPPORT

RIXSON 370 (SEE

C 2" x 1" x 1/8" DRILLED & TAPPED TO
REC. 1/4 x 1/4 x 3/16" GLASS STOP.

1/4" x 10½" STL PLATE DRILLED AS REQ'D
TO ACCOMODATE LOCKCASE.

1/4" x 1½" FLAT FOR BOX FRAME

1/4" x 8" PLATE NOTCHED AS REQ'D
TO ACCOMODATE RECESSED LATCH LEVER

YALE 8601 FL MORTISE PASSAGE SET
W/ BRONZE-PLATED ARMOR FRONT &
LEVER HANDLE ARCADIA ARR IN BRONZE

L 1/4" x 1/4" x 3/16"

3/8" CLEAR LAMINATED SAFETY GLASS
SET IN RUBBER GASKET W/IN
GLAZING TROUGH.

BOTTOM PORTION OF RIXSON 370 PIVOT
HINGE W/IN C 2 x 1 x 1/8 PLATE FOR SAME
SHALL BE MORTISE SET W/IN FLOOR
TO MAINTAIN 1/4" CLEARANCE FOR DOOR
@ FLOOR.

1/4" x 2" STL FLAT FLUSH W/ FLOOR & WELDED
TO DOOR JAMBS. SAME TO BE NOTCHED
FOR HINGE INSTALLATION.

C 2 x 1 x 1/8 WELDED TO FLAT 1 1/4" x 1/4"
GLAZING SUPPORT.

1/8" x 1 1/4" CONTINUOUS STL. GUIDE TO SLIDE
W/IN TRACK OF (2) CUT 7/8 x 7/8 x 1/8.

The whole abstractly reflects the composition and elegance of a Mapplethorpe photograph: selected parts of the architecture are portrayed with absolute clarity, and surface layers of ordinary materials become extraordinary by their isolation.

The foundation is the locus of the community of people impacted by the life and work of Robert Mapplethorpe. In the middle of its space is a living area. Undefined by any specific function or activity, this living area is the symbolic center of the foundation. To one side of this area, a thick wall holds the photographic archives. Set against the plaster face of this wall, a wood ledge accommodates in a simple manner a limited display of photographs, which are changed on a regular basis.

MATERIALS: European beech veneer, steamed and flat cut; smooth-troweled plaster, with graphite; cast-iron column, existing; carriage beam, fir, existing; red oak floor, industrial #2, existing; lighting fixtures by IIOO Architect

GREENWICH VILLAGE DUPLEX
New York, New York, 1990

In an era of transience, an architecture of continuity develops not from deep knowledge of one epoch, one e *ation of many. Multiplicity provides the freedom to create a new collectivity from disparate elements and to*

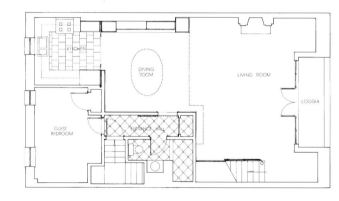

The clients, two painters, desired a home whose architecture would express continuity and permanence, qualities increasingly absent in mediated popular culture.

culture, but rather through the fresh consider-
ence to places outside of time and self.

Our clients urged us to use every inch of the small, 1,500-square-foot apartment. In fact, they saw the design process as similar to that undertaken for a ship, where every bit of space is put to some use. In this vein, a traditional Japanese practice of locating storage areas beneath a stair provided a beautiful source of inspiration. We adapted the idea, maximizing the efficiency of the stair.

Our sketches for the newel post of the stair railing were suggestive of an attenuated club; they lingered until we looked seriously at baseball bats. Our search for the right one ended at the archetype—the last model used by Babe Ruth. Its slender handle and swollen barrel appear at the base of the stair, signed and cast in bronze.

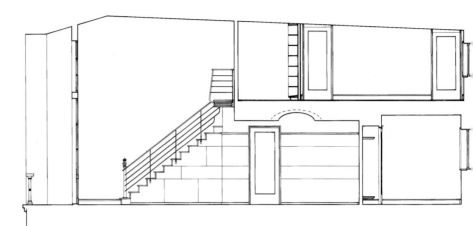

The architectural investigation began through a series of schematic elevations, with attention to qualities of surface and color. These elevations breached the disparate scales of the "large" and "small" halves of the apartment, and did not achieve an affective whole. The lack of an integrative component was remedied with the use of leaves of poplar veneer paneling. Sequenced to suggest taut fabric and to maintain tactility in the surface, the panels clad the base of the stair, continue through the dining room, and reemerge into the two-story living room. This layer of wood, detailed to disguise its thinness, envelops the space with a surface that enhances its integrity in three dimensions.

New, milled poplar is a pronounced shade of green that changes over time to violet brown. This color is unpleasant without intervention, so we soaked the panels with lime-green aniline dye. Now altered, the change in the color of the poplar is less predictable and more delightful.

We endeavor to place ourselves out of time in our work, guided by images both actual and metaphoric, as well as by personal experience. This approach is productive only if we remain grounded in the real constituents of program and technical requirements. We are committed to the process of construction: it has its own dialogue consisting of the appropriate use of materials, the details by which they are assembled, and the expertise of the craftspeople who complete the work.

seek a nonspecific consciousness in the work, inspired by the beauty and pleasure of aesthetic experience.

The selection of materials, and the color of each, is coded according to the role of the material. Each substance has its own tonal predisposition and aging process, which we consider thoughtfully in assembling the collection of materials for the work. One layer of architecture is expressed by the sensuous combination of hues that change with the passage of time.

MEDIA WALL
New York, New York, 1990

The specter and fact of media often educe ambivalence and duplicity. In constructing an architecture that contains

iums of media, we favor their dissimulation, a response, of course, to the dissemination of media in the domicile.

GREENWICH VILLAGE TOWNHOUSE
New York, New York, 1991

The adaptation of an apartment building into a single-family house entailed processes of addition as well as subtraction. The nature of our intervention was deliberately ambiguous.

Transformation is a natural outcome of reconstruction. The combination of extant conditions, structural change, and new occupancy may be multifarious, but not necessarily complex.

Our aim was to refrain from giving the building an atmosphere of newness. Thus, on the second floor, in creating one opening for three doors from what were two windows, we borrowed the form of arched door openings inside the room as a continuous motif. By blurring the distinction between preexisting materials and details and new ones, we made unclear what we added and what we removed.

The work cannot be totally predetermined; it often develops in directions different from those planned. External events continually contribute to the evolution of 1100 projects. We integrate these circumstances into a coherent whole.

Materials and finishes, and the processes of working with them, are highly interdependent and subject to change. After opening the kitchen and adjacent dining area by completely rebuilding the first floor of the house, we installed a new surface of green concrete and inlaid slabs of bluestone from the backyard. Prior to sealing the freshly poured floor, muriatic acid was used to clean it. Fumes from the acid rose and caused a thin film of rust to form on the newly installed pressed metal ceiling, removing its sheen. This turn of events changed the character of the space in an unexpected but, in our view, not unwelcome fashion.

The client knew of enormous marble fireplace walls from his travels. He wanted to import some to install in this house until we advised him they would not fit in the building. Instead, we designed this fireplace in collaboration with him; it is made of dyed concrete, cast in molds piece by piece, and brought into the house from a sculptor's workshop in New Jersey.

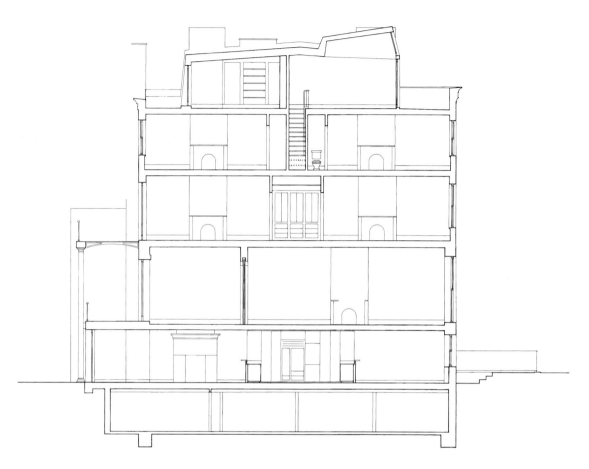

Originally the building was a tightly contained five-story structure. We opened it and extended it wherever possible, preserving, however, the landmarked street front. At the roof level, we made terraces from attic poché, and we added a terrace to the third level. Made of glass, this terrace admits light to the level below, itself another terrace that stands atop an extension of the first level toward the rear garden.

Tinted concrete tiles, found by the client, were used throughout the house.

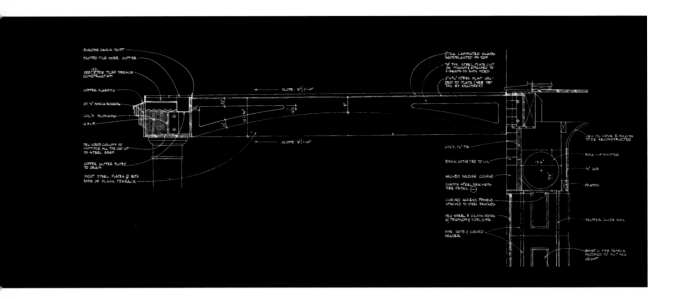

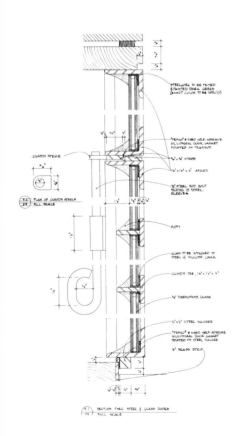

ESPRIT DE CORP
New York, New York, 1992

The pursuit of the ready-to-wear customer (and of fashion's imprimatur) is weighted with paradox: the need to be all things to all customers, and the importance of conveying one specific image to one specific customer. *In a time of multiple contradictions, we choose neither to favor one constituent over another nor to effect balance amid opposition. We confront each set of contradictions we encounter and investigate its potential expression within the language of architecture.* At Esprit, a complex program was the product of inherent ambiguities: the need for two different showrooms (with a single point of entry) and the desire for varied scales—grandeur on one hand, intimacy on the other. We addressed these contradictions, manifesting them through the juxtaposition of space (fixed, yet flexible), materials (immutable, yet variable), and light (direct, yet remote).

Light extends in all directions of the work, befitting a matrix: laterally from perimeter windows through translucent glass transom walls; and vertically from skylights through glass floors. The plan gives an incomplete description of the character of the spaces, and in certain instances is altogether deceiving. The presence of daylight in the interiors belies the breadth of the facility and the comparative remove of some functions from the exterior windows. More significant is the role of daylight in architecture; here it integrates the project across three dimensions.

Suffusing a space with light is one part of its transformation from construction to architecture. We play with natural light—transposing, transmuting, modulating, manipulating it—in the process of creating space.

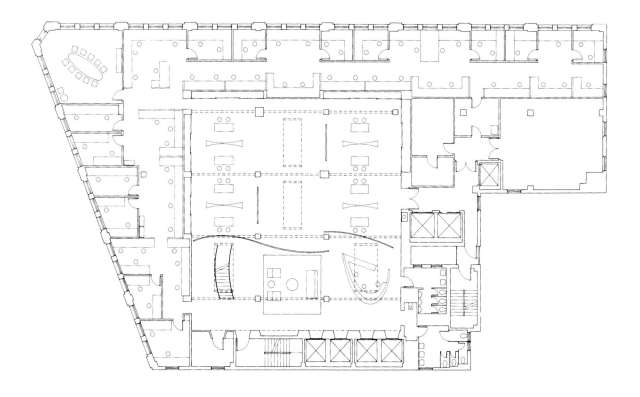

We believe in the signific

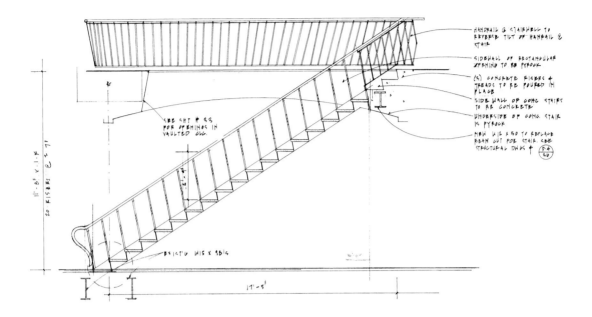

ransitions between materials and spaces. For us, transitional moments enrich and strengthen the experience of architecture.

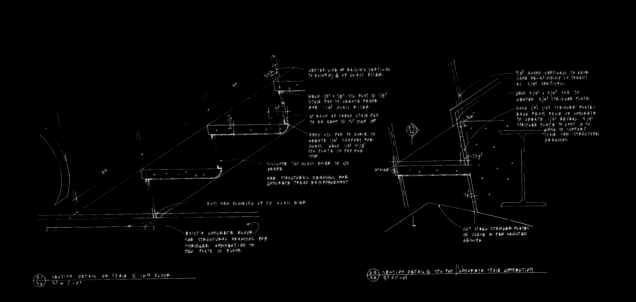

Inspired by the idea of a bazaar in the development of the plan, we imagined its vitality an essential counterpoint to the rational and regular column bays. The functions of clothing display and presentation were conceived as screens, capable of being moved in response not only to the client's desire for infinitely flexible space, but our desire that these components float within the architectural envelope. However, absolute flexibility is a fallacy. The making of architecture is a process that, by definition and fact, demands that hard decisions be made out of constraints, parameters, requirements, in short, that things be pinned down.

The thoughtful modulation of qualities of light—incisive focus, lustrous glow, sustained warm

Compelled by the lowness, the flatness of the space, we added a series of vaults that, while lowering the ceiling, enhanced the scale of the site and brought order and consistency to the project. The paradoxical quality of this move offers more than a reflection of the contradictions inherent in the project. It is evidence, in the elegant disposition of pragmatic concerns within its curvature, of an integration of irony and utility.

by extension, space itself, is the aim of the play with natural light.

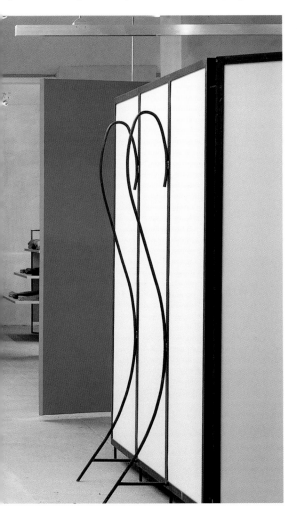

Coated with a sound-absorptive mixture of plaster and gypsum, the ceiling contains a precise pattern of recessed display lamps. Ambient light from suspended fixtures reflects off the surface of the ceiling, producing a diffuse and even light in the space. The volume created between the flat slab of the structure above and the hung curve of the vault is used as a pressurized plenum for the air-conditioning system, as well as for the concealment of the fire detection and sound systems.

RESERVOIR HOUSE
Westchester County, New York, 1994

The site is spectacular. It is approached by a long, beguiling drive from a main road. Visible at the end of the drive is the crest of a steep slope, the side of which had been dotted with a string of cottages concealed by the peak of the slope. At the foot of the hill, only a short distance away, is a lake, formerly a reservoir.

Architecture builds on precedents. We effect architectural continuities through the integration of our work with its antecedents.

The original structure on this property was a one-room stone cottage that sheltered a pump attendant. Partially embedded in the slope of the hill, the cottage had been enlarged laterally, and the changes ignored the integrity of the fieldstone walls. In building a new house on top of the old one, we "raised" the house and its profile, gave the building a presence at the end of the driveway, constructed space for the public functions of the house, and unified an otherwise disparate assemblage of structures below.

The new building incorporates a number of different conditions into its foundation: flat terrain, sloping blue ledge, walls of the original structure. We wanted old new materials to be harmonized, yet at the same time ognizably separate.

The work is built on the basis of modern prece
Toward this end, we differentiated the roof from the by inserting a discrete band of material: stucco was us above the stone walls, and cedar above the shingled The broad overhang of the roof enhances the percep of this separation.

materials and elements of architecture are rationally and distinctly expressed.

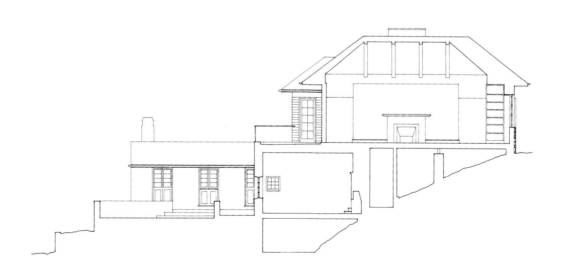

The lower level accommodates the bedroom suites. At the south end is the master wing, which encompasses two previous additions; at the north end is the guest wing, which includes the original stone cottage structure.

definition of space may be created as much by ceilings as by walls. A section and a plan work together to describe architecture.

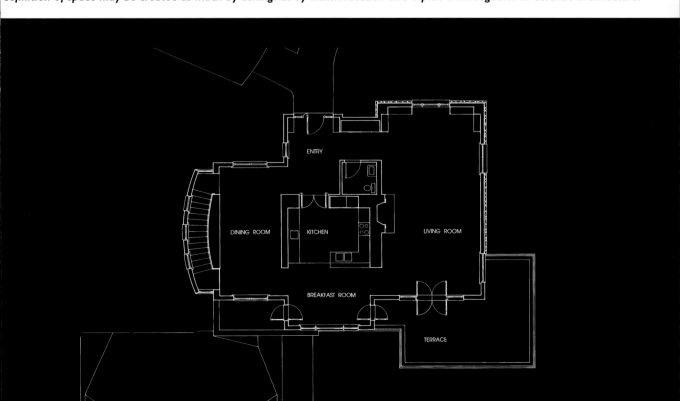

ENTRY

DINING ROOM   KITCHEN   LIVING ROOM

BREAKFAST ROOM

TERRACE

GEORGES HOUSE
Katonah, New York, 1993 (project)

Although this project did not progress beyond the schematic
design phase, we remain committed to the ideas explored there
and to the objectives we set out to accomplish. The project was
to be more than simply an addition; it was, in fact, a new
house. We intended this new building to be a strong contrast to
the original house, a separate part of a larger whole.

*At 1100, the work evolves out of an interaction between architect and client, and also between architects.
Invention often occurs with the meeting of two minds, two perspectives.*

The house was meant to connect two generations in the family
of five that would occupy it. Thus both the new house and the
existing house were to share common materials.

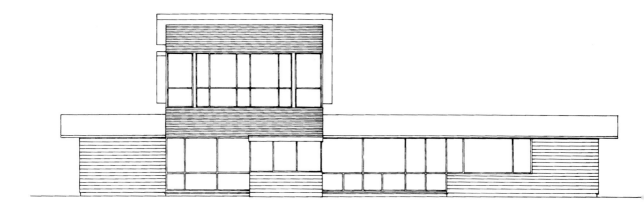

With the work left unrealized, we return to it and ask ourselves
if the design holds together. As time passes and our experience
broadens, we recognize room for improvement.

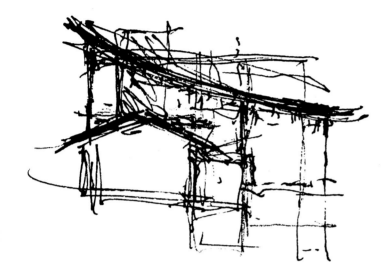

The project began out of the parents' need for some space of their own: a bedroom and a studio. The long building (the original house) would be given over to the children's bedrooms; we respected the clients' wish to change it as little as possible. Portions of the new house, therefore, ultimately rest on the grade beams of the existing structure and renovations are confined to the needy parts of the original building.

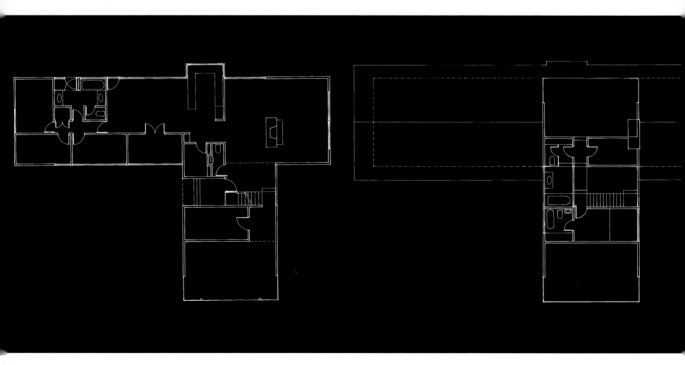

The point of integration occurs as the two public rooms of the original house are literally coopted by the new house. We expressed the new structure as a dynamic and vibrant counterpoint to the stasis of the original house, especially in the form of the roof. The intention was for the disparate forms to work together.

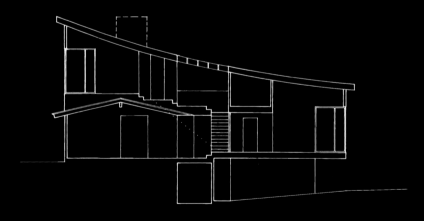

THE ROBBINS OFFICE
New York, New York, 1994

The site, on a corner, receives brilliant light from the south and west. From the interior of the office, there are spectacular views down Park Avenue. We were asked to make an office for a literary agent dedicated as much to the hard business of getting books published as to making a place where writers would feel at ease.

Architecture can suggest the enclosure, rhythm, and unfolding of a good book. In making architecture, our primary concern is not with telling a story, but in making space for discovery to occur.

The display and storage of books was clearly a critical part of the program. We devised two strategies for presentation and storage through the use of two parallel walls of books. One is solid, continuous, and plainly on view to the common space in the office; it is constructed of painted wood shelving, and is entirely utilitarian. The other wall is segmented, disguised by dyed wooden cases. Although held apart from one another, the cases form an interdependent relationship with other architectural elements in the project; they support the glass and the doors around them.

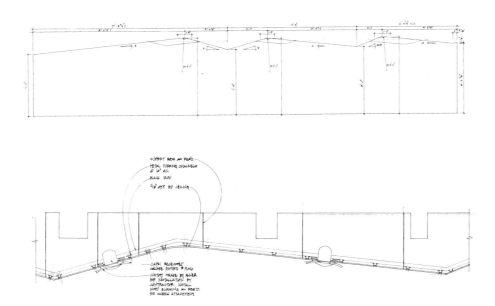

The work becomes abstract through the clear presentation of its elements and materials.
Out of the adjacencies and combinations of elements and materials emerges the architecture.

Architecture that is expressed in the most elemental terms demands the most rigorous detailing. We believe rigor is more often effected in straightforward, as opposed to complicated, methods of connection and assembly. Although the best solution for a detail is not always the easiest one to build, it necessarily preserves the integrity of the material(s) and, by extension, of the architecture.

TSE
New York, New York, 1994

Among the ideas we tested in this work was a desire to effect a radiance within the space, by means of the suffusion of light inside the store and its corresponding glow outside. Through a manipulation of basic principles of light behavior, we explored an expansion of its role in the character of architecture.

We cannot identify a specific formula for sensuality in architecture; we discover it, a sensibility that emerges by design, from the dialogue between materials, shape, light, and hue.

The first street-level store for TSE provides an elegant display environment for a range of unique, luxurious, cashmere and cashmere-blend clothing. Light originating from a tortoise-shell-shaped chandelier casts a warm, inviting glow in the vitrinelike store. The two-story entrance announces the essence of the shop in one glance.

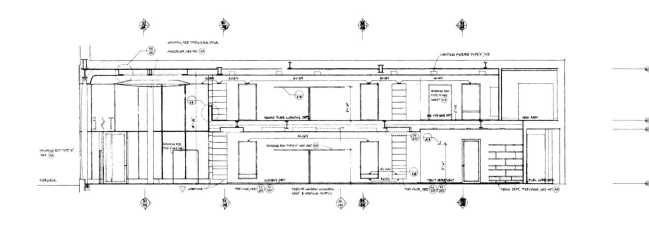

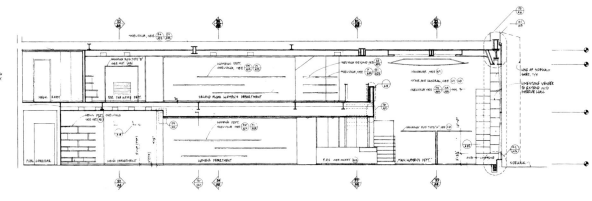

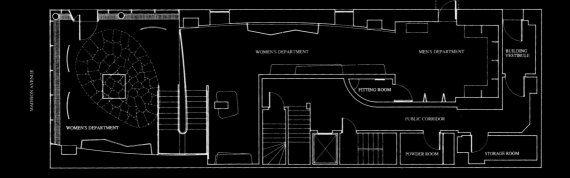

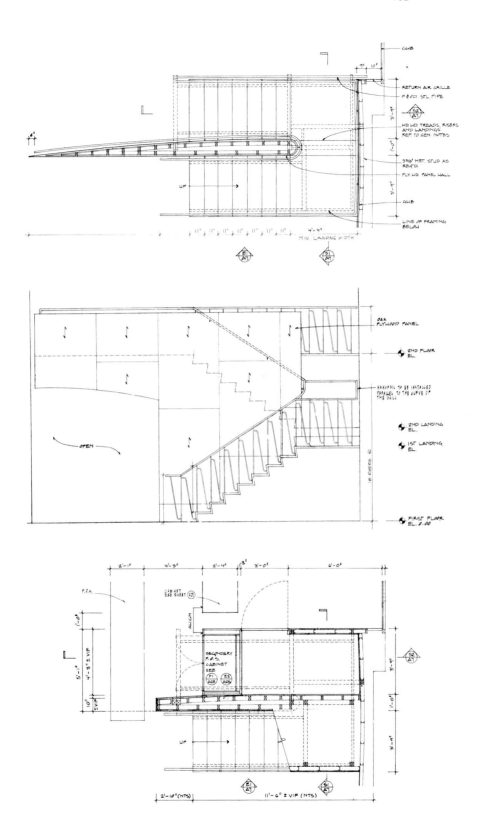

We believe architecture is best marked by a facile coalescence of dissimilar materials. Such a synthesis offers sensations, both visual and tactile, that may introduce an architecture of sensuality.

In a modern mixing of materials, the cashmere in this clothing is frequently used in combination with as many as eighteen other yarns. While soft, warm, and beautiful, it, like all materials, has its limitations. The subtle elegance of cashmere has a recessive affect on its presentation, and it does not hang well; it is best seen and stored folded. Nonetheless, it served as inspiration for the architecture, leading us toward an exploration of new uses for materials that are familiar to us. The fabric is displayed throughout the store, on a mixture of materials—curved beech shelves, stacked planes of glass, and thin bent steel rods.

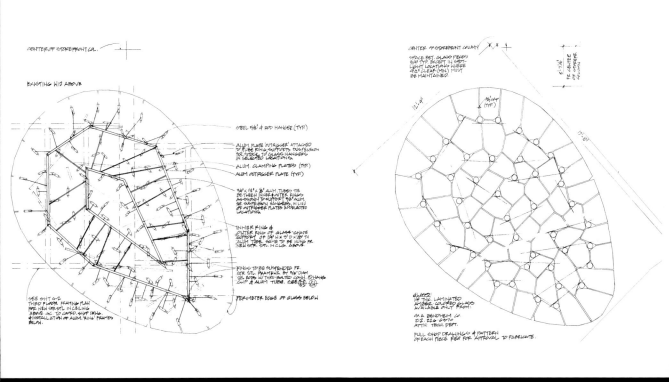

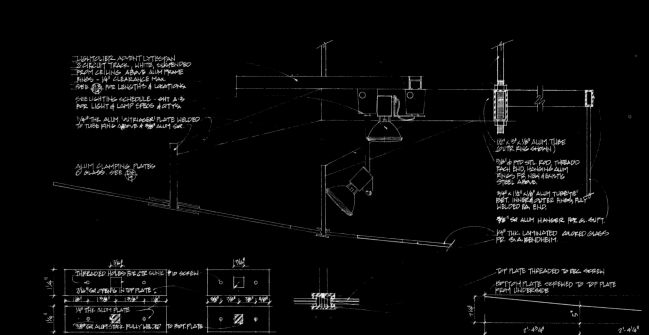

SCHWARZ-TUCHSCHERER HOUSE

Heuchelheim, Germany, 1996

The process of the work is informed by subtle interpretations of circumscribed conditions, cultural predispositions, and our patient inclination to distort a type.
Located in a small town outside Frankfurt, this house reinterprets traditional German village architecture within its own context. Views to the countryside beyond recall time past; views within the new house look to time present and future. Strict building codes dictated the size and shape of the house, the method of construction, and even the slope and type of roof. Operating within these rules, we designed a house for a young family that incorporates a professional office for the practice of physical therapy.

Federal regulations further prescribed the amount of space for the business of physical therapy, and thereby had an impact on the arrangement of the house. We took advantage of the gently sloping site by embedding the office into it and hiding it from direct view. This left a unified volume above the ground for the domestic functions of the house.

The wood and glass wing of the living and dining areas wraps around one corner of the south facade. In a gesture to its orientation toward a valley beyond, the roof tilts in two directions; this also emphasizes its intersection with the main volume of the house. Finally, this manner of inclination permits the introduction of a small window at the corner, which brings light into a second-story bedroom.

SCHWARZ-TUCHSCHERER HOUSE

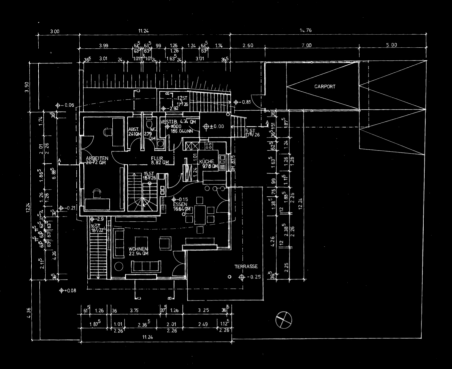

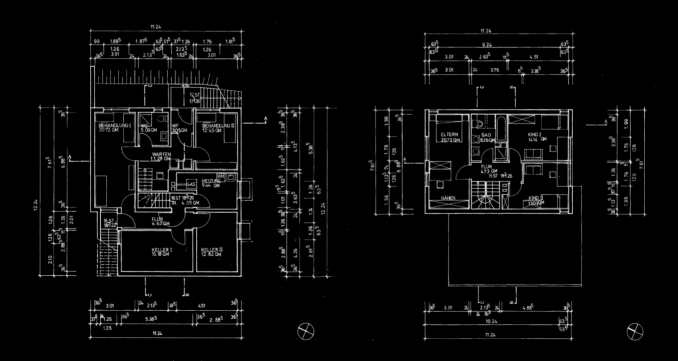

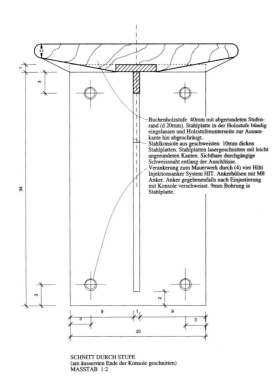

Buchenholzstufe 40mm mit abgerundeten Stufen-
rand (d 20mm). Stahlplatte in der Holzstufe bündig
eingelassen und Holzstufenunterseite zur Aussen-
kante hin abgeschrägt.
Stahlkonsole aus geschweissten 10mm dicken
Stahlplatten. Stahlplatten lasergeschnitten mit leicht
angerundeten Kanten. Sichtbare durchgängige
Schweissnaht entlang der Anschlüsse.
Verankerung zum Mauerwerk durch (4) vier Hilti
Injektionsanker System HIT. Ankerhülsen mit M8
Anker. Anker gegebenenfalls nach Einjustierung
mit Konsole verschweisst. 9mm Bohrung in
Stahlplatte.

SCHNITT DURCH STUFE
(am äussersten Ende der Konsole geschnitten)
MASSTAB 1:2

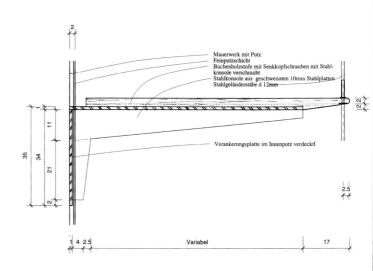

Mauerwerk mit Putz
Feinputzschicht
Buchenholzstufe mit Senkkopfschrauben mit Stahl-
konsole verschraubt
Stahlkonsole aus geschweissten 10mm Stahlplatten
Stahlgeländerstäbe d 12mm

Verankerungsplatte im Innenputz verdecktl

Variabel

We find an indication of freedom in the exploration of the expressive and functional capacities of common materials.

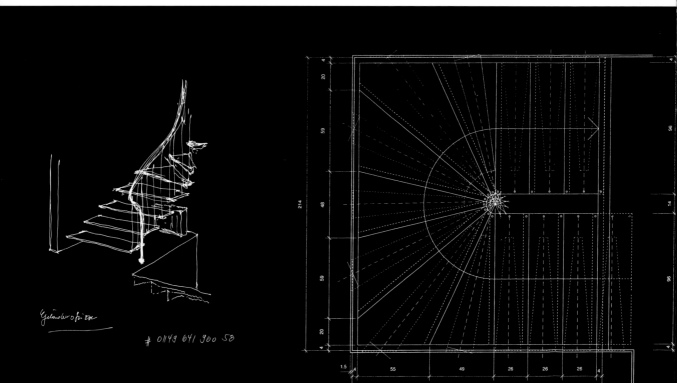

HM/FM HOUSE
Truro, Massachusetts, 1996

The design of this house, a vacation home for a family with two children, began with a simple, sculptural idea: the intersection of two volumes, one grounded (HM), the other aloft (FM). This latter volume is cantilevered and engages the grounded volume in a dialogue of form and material. Symbolic of two different aesthetics, the volumes are, in effect, two halves of a whole. A matrix of ideas based on various systems—structural, methodological, and economic—completes the architectural strategies for the making of the house.

There is reason behind our experimentation; it is directed toward testing—not erasing—boundaries, particularly those of material and linguistic expression of a given typology.

The 56 standard prefabricated wood windows (32 operable, 24 fixed) and 8 custom-fabricated wood-and-glass doors equal 22 percent of the exterior surface area of the house.

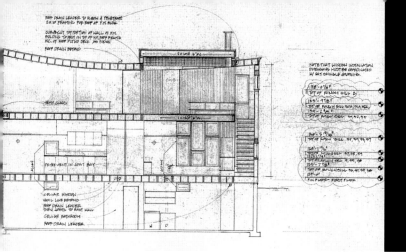

sixteen-by-forty-four-foot rectangle outlines the grounded building, permitting a simple process of excavation; the sixteen-foot dimension permits a clear span of two-by-twelves for the floor decks. While the plan is a generative force in the design, it is indeterminate without sections and elevations. The siding of the HM building is Eastern white cedar shingles with two five-course bands of Western red cedar shingles; the FM building is clad with vertical-grain Western redwood. The materials will weather with time as the building takes its place in the landscape.

The house is sited on a hillcrest overlooking Cape Cod Bay. The local architecture ranges from vernacular gable-roofed "Capes" to recently built "contemporaries" and reflects the diverse interests of the populace.

Surprises often reveal themselves when we examine each part of the whole separately.

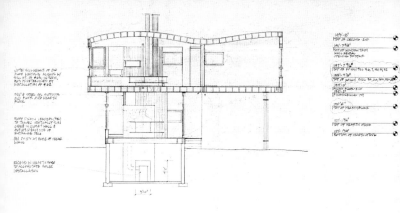

To build the house within the lexicon of frame construction, yet complete the original notion of holding
a portion of the building aloft, became a significant
challenge in the design process. The second level is
both engaged and disengaged from the floor of the
grounded building below. The staircase—a series of
cantilevered and staggered wooden boxes—extends
this duality. Space, and the circulation of cellar-
cooled air, passes from the subterranean level to the
second level of both of the buildings through the
open construction of the staircase.

MATERIALS: Portland cement-stucco; vertical-grain select red fir;
Homasote panels; hot-rolled steel plate and pipe; Douglas fir battens;
white cedar planks; birch-veneer plywood; Medex particle board
(soaked with aniline dye); gypsum wall board

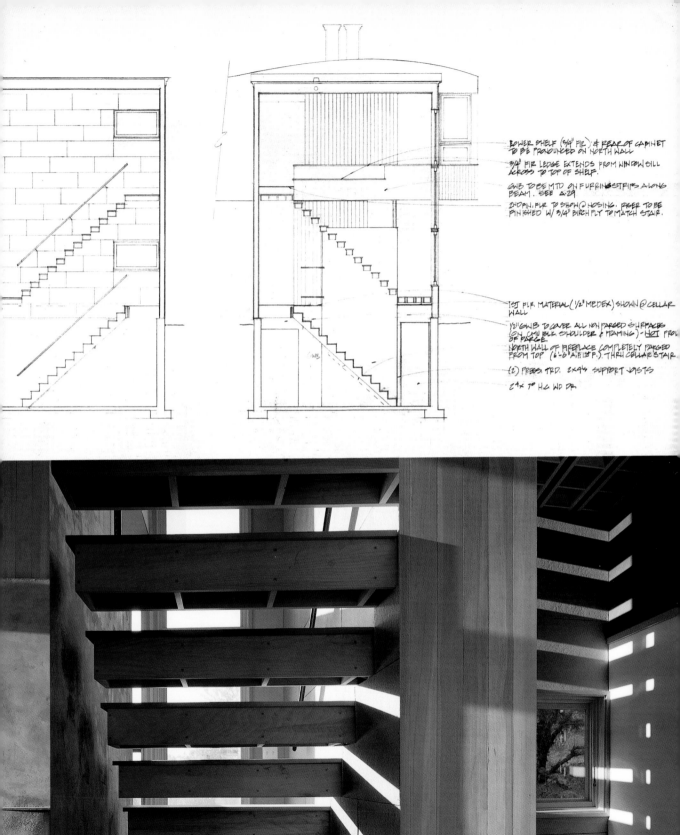

LOWER SHELF (3/4" FIR.) & REAR OF CABINET TO BE PRONOUNCED ON NORTH WALL

3/4" FIR LEDGE EXTENDS FROM WINDOW SILL ACROSS TO TOP OF SHELF.

GWB TO BE M'TD ON FURRING STRIPS ALONG BEAM. SEE A-29

2'-0" FIN. FLR. TO SHOW @ NOSING. RISER TO BE FINISHED W/ 3/4" BIRCH PLY TO MATCH STAIR.

1ST FLR. MATERIAL (1/2" MEDEX) SHOWN @ CELLAR WALL

1/2" GWB TO COVER ALL NON PARGED SURFACES (ON CMU BLK. SHOULDER & FRAMING) - NOT PROL OF PARGE.
NORTH WALL OF FIREPLACE COMPLETELY PARGED FROM TOP (6'-6" A/F. 1ST F.P.) THRU CELLAR STAIR.

(2) PRESS. TRD. 2x4's SUPPORT JOISTS

2'-4" x 7'-0" H.C. WD. DR.

movement of space and passage of light between inside and outside are the precepts for a permeable architecture.

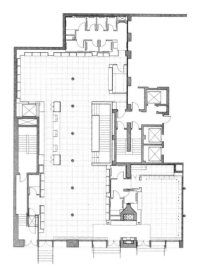

J.CREW
New York, New York, 1996

Our work for J.Crew is based on a prototypical store we developed in 1995 with the design director of the company, David Schaefer. In the prototype, we implemented subtle but significant changes to reinvigorate the already clean line present in their earlier stores and displays. This store in Soho carries the process to its mature expression.

To be direct without being reductive or severe is to effect clarity in design, an essence of 1100 architecture.

The site of the store, in a historic district known in the last two decades for its multitude of art galleries, influenced the presentation of the merchandise and the way we conceived of the architecture. A staircase, cantilevered into a slender opening in the center of the site, ensures an active dialogue between the main and lower levels of the store.

The areas of the store that present various product classifications are defined through subtle architectural means, a strategy appropriate to a project typology that requires almost uninterrupted views throughout the space. Ceiling coffers and lighting systems, precisely arranged, accomplish this task. Wood cabinetry—painted and unpainted—is built into the walls and allows selective groupings of merchandise. These elements are designed to recede from the product, leaving it as the principal occupant of the space.

STAIRCASE: concealed steel-beam frame, steel-plate carriage stringers, cast-iron treads, milled cold-rolled steel spindles, maple handrail; total dead-load weight: 5.47 tons

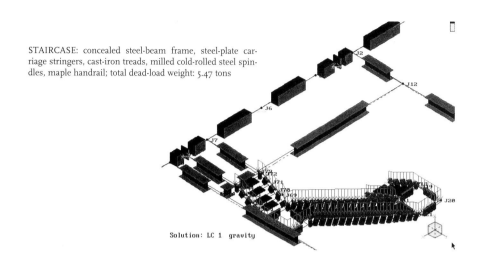

Solution: LC 1 gravity

The perception of weightlessness is a delicate and subtle but, we believe, essential sensation of an experience in architecture.

RIFKIN RESIDENCE
New York, New York, 1996

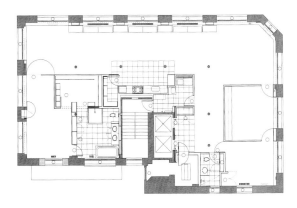

The design of this apartment was informed by two points of departure—the plan and the perimeter wall—and their confluence. The plan is marked by the freestanding columns of the building's internal structure. Exploiting their fixed positions, we used the columns as an ordonnance against which we assembled the functions of the program.

The construction of a place of memory is not a historical exercise but a process of abstraction. Abstraction avoids sentimentality and allows the object of memory to be reconceived more simply as an integrated part of a new whole.

We encourage our clients to find a method of communication that will convey to us their desires and predilections. Descriptive adjectives work for some, tearing pictures from magazines works for others. Here, over one hundred images were presented as things, places, colors to consider (or avoid). Extracting essential qualities from this selection of images infused the work with the clients' personalities.

Architecture built on memory does not always remember. A new place in the present selectively effaces the pa

Our concern for retaining the original character of the perimeter wall was so great that we first proposed to leave it intact, except for the windows. We saw that wall as an abstract and flat plane, unaffected by our interventions in other parts of the space. As the project evolved, however, it became apparent that a visual connection between windows and wall was necessary. So we inserted a recurring ledge of concrete—both a windowsill and a horizontal line interacting with the solid vertical planes of wall between the windows.

SOHO LOFT
New York, New York, 1996

Autonomy and horizontality are focal points for the work. A level plane represents the abundant potential of a surface that is coterminous with, yet independent from, the influence of other elements.

METRO PICTURES

New York, New York, 1997

We seek to effect instances of suspension in the work. They stimulate us on many levels, not least for their perceptual contradicti

...e realities of the work: the construction of a well-built and meaningful architecture.

The entrance is the determinative point in the design of this gallery. It exploits its exposure to the street with glass panels that offer a view to three axes of the project. Beyond the threshold, the enfilade arrangement of the exhibition spaces is immediately discernible, establishing a visual hierarchy that initiates the spatial experience. To the right of the entrance, the visitors' desk effectively extends the front wall in a direction perpendicular to the main axis of the gallery. Meanwhile, a cantilevered staircase introduces a vital third, vertical, axis, offering access to additional exhibition space and offices on the upper level.

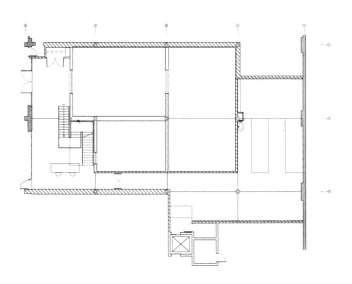

Architecture benefits from places without a specific function; they are often the most essential, the ones we need and use most.

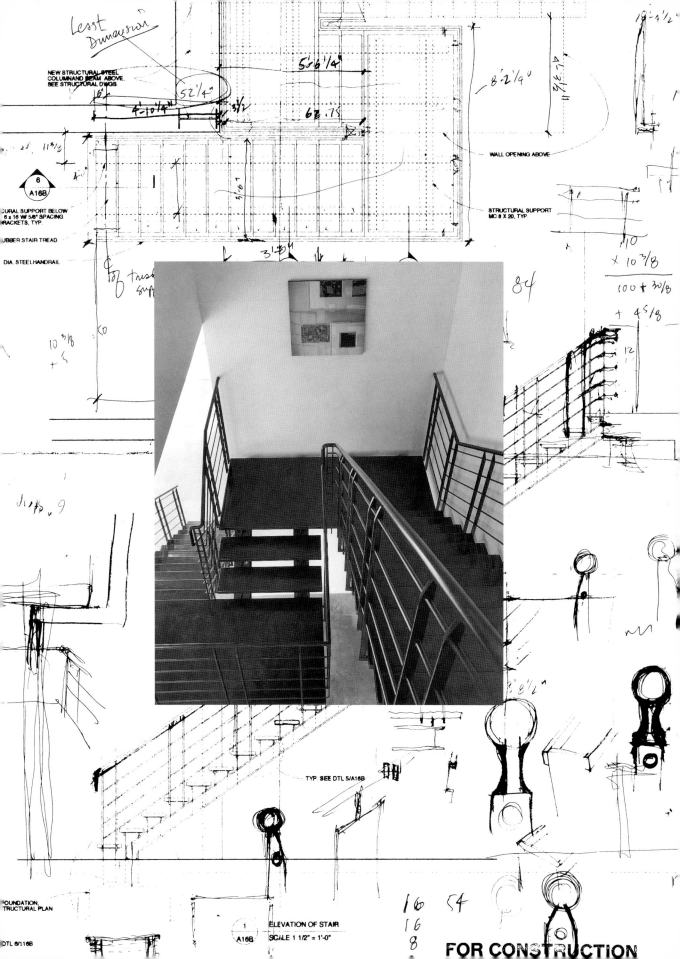

Less Dimension

NEW STRUCTURAL STEEL
COLUMN AND BEAM ABOVE.
SEE STRUCTURAL DWGS.

52¼"

5'-6¼"

4'-10¼"   3½

6½.75

8'-2⅛"

4'-3½

WALL OPENING ABOVE

11³/₈

6
A16B

...CURAL SUPPORT BELOW
... 6 x 16 W/ 5/8" SPACING
...RACKETS, TYP.

...UBBER STAIR TREAD

...DIA. STEEL HANDRAIL

STRUCTURAL SUPPORT
MC 8 X 20, TYP.

3½'4

84

X 10³/₈

100 + 30/8

+ 4⁵/₈

12

10³/₈
+ 5

TYP SEE DTL 5/A16B

16   54
16
8

...FOUNDATION,
...TRUCTURAL PLAN

1
A16B

ELEVATION OF STAIR

SCALE 1 1/2" = 1'-0"

DTL 6/116B

FOR CONSTRUCTION

LITTLE RED SCHOOL HOUSE &
ELISABETH IRWIN HIGH SCHOOL
New York, New York, 1997

An addition to a school, this new building will occupy a parcel of land on the Avenue of the Americas. It is bordered on two sides by existing school facilities and on a third by a six-story apartment building. The exterior elevation presents a new entrance to the middle division of the school but does not imitate the converted row house to which it connects. Instead it effects a transition from a building of a typically large, urban scale to a more intimate environment suitable for developing young people.

We build for communities and their constituents. Even as the nature of this constituency may vary, our mission does not: to make a positive impact on people and the purpose and consciousness of their lives.

Within the compact structure, there is a cluster of rooms that answers to a diverse program: a new library, a technology classroom, two art studios, and a new cafeteria and commons. The building mediates between two of the school's existing facilities, improving the flow of circulation across disparate floor levels and making a unified complex.

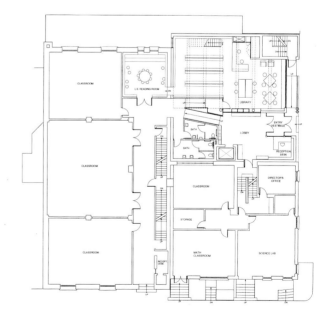

182

LIST OF PROJECTS
1986–1997

1983 • Bryan Hunt Loft, New York • 1984 • Furniture of the Twentieth Century, New York • Blum Helman Gallery Warehouse, New York • Henri Bendel, New York • Indochine, New York • 1985 • Duchin Hayward Residence, New York • Sultan Residence, New York • Sultan Studio, New York • 1986 • **Exhibition of Selected Work, Frankfurt, Germany** • **Orleans House, Cape Cod, Mass.** • **Hatch House, New York** • Mahoney Residence, New York • Hutchins Residence, New York • Page Residence, New York (project) • 1987 • Hawks Residence, New York • Wolff Gallery, New York • Breit Residence, Jersey City, N.J. • 1988 • Sultan Residence, Sag Harbor, N.Y. (project) • Mahoney/Pardoe Residence, New York • Cooper/McRae Residence, New York • 1989 • **West Village Residence, New York** • **New Festival Theater, New York (project)** • **Upper East Side Townhouse, New York (project)** • **A/D Gallery, New York** • Scholder Loft, New York • Blitz Residence, New York • Pedowitz Residence, New York • Charisma Records, New York • Salle Studio, New York • Nichols/Sawyer Residence, New York (project) • 1990 • **Bleckner Studio and Residence, New York** • **The Robert Mapplethorpe Foundation, New York** • **Greenwich Village Duplex, New York** • **Media Wall, New York** • D'Offay Gallery, New York • Sultan Residence, New York • Driade, New York • Fogel Residence, Washington, Conn. (project) • 1991 • **Greenwich Village Townhouse, New York** • West Village Residence, New York • 1992 • **Esprit de Corp, New York** • Byrne/Lutz Townhouse, New York • 1993 • **Georges House, Katonah, N.Y. (project)** • D'Orazio Residence, New York • Mademoiselle, New York • Esprit de Corp Shop Concept • Susie Tompkins Shop Concept • Esprit Macy's Store, New York • Susie Tompkins Macy's Store, New York • Revlon, New York • Liz Claiborne Shop Concept • Uchino Shop Concept, Japan • 1994 • **Reservoir House, Westchester County, N.Y.** • **The Robbins Office, New York** • **TSE, New York** • New World Entertainment, New York • SW Networks, New York • Merkley Newman Harty, New York (project) • Riggio Residence, Bridgehampton • Capitol Records, New York • 1995 • TSE Woodbury, N.Y. • TSE Napa Valley, Calif. • TSE Shop Concept • J.Crew—Bellevue, Seattle • J.Crew—Tysons, Va. • Sharp Residence, New York (project) • Vitrashop Shop Fixtures, Weil am Rhein, Germany • Riggio Residence, New York (project) • 1996 • **Schwarz-Tuchscherer House, Heuchelheim, Germany** • **HM/FM House, Truro, Mass.** • **J.Crew—Prince Street, New York** • **Rifkin Residence, New York** • **Soho Loft, New York** • Morrow/Bibler Barn, Woodville, R.I. • Turlington Townhouse, New York • Perry Corporation Offices, New York • Perry Residence, New York • Barish Residence, New York (project) • 1997 • **Metro Pictures, New York** • **Little Red School House & Elisabeth Irwin High School, New York** • J.Crew—Fifth Avenue, New York • J.Crew—Short Hills, N.J. • J.Crew—Boca Raton, Fla. • J.Crew—Century City, Calif. • Delany/Staso Townhouse, New York • Woods Residence, New York • Blue Ridge Capital Offices, New York • Rene Lezard, New York • Abell Duplex, New York • Jerome Residence, New York • Shahid & Co. Offices, New York • Saint Francis College, Brooklyn, N.Y.

(Projects in **bold** are featured in this book.)

1100 PERSONNEL
1986–1997

Javier Arizmendi (Robbins, TSE) • Rafael Berkowitz (Esprit) • Sarah Botts • Patricia Brett (Georges, Robbins) • Mary Heath Carpenter (Hatch, W. V. Residence, E. S. Townhouse, A/D, Bleckner, Mapplethorpe, G. V. Duplex, G. V. Townhouse, Esprit, Reservoir) • Jeremy Carvalho (TSE) • Walter Chatham (Exhibition, Hatch) • Noel Clarke (Esprit, Georges, TSE) • Gwen Connors (Bleckner, Esprit, Robbins, TSE) • Miriam Corti • Brendan Cotter (Schwarz, HM/FM, J.Crew, Rifkin, Little Red) • Lia Debigoropoulou (W. V. Residence) • Katherine DeFehr (Soho Loft) • Sarah Evans Dunn • Mary Beth Elliott (Hatch, W. V. Residence) • Ines Elskop (Exhibition, Hatch, W. V. Residence, New Festival, E. S. Townhouse, A/D, Bleckner, Mapplethorpe, G. V. Duplex) • Barbara Eyland • Martin Felsen • Jose Gabriel Fernandez • Martin Fetner (Hatch) • Morgan Fleming • Jean-Pierre Frey (G. V. Duplex) • Erica Friedland (HM/FM, Little Red) • James Gettinger (TSE) • Inge Gottschling (Little Red) • Maria Gray (Metro) • Tobias Grimminger (Little Red) • Judith Gross • Leslie Jill Hanson • Gordon Haslett (Mapplethorpe, G. V. Townhouse) • Andrea Hilger (HM/FM) • Eva Hillenhinrichs (TSE, Schwarz, HM/FM) • Joachim Hopp (Little Red) • Alex Hurst (TSE) • Bruce Irwin (Soho Loft, Metro) • Laurence Jaquet (Bleckner, G. V. Duplex, Media Wall, G. V. Townhouse, Esprit, Robbins) • Tom Kowalski (Bleckner) • Carmen Lenzi (Reservoir, Georges, Robbins, TSE, HM/FM, J.Crew, Metro, Little Red) • Mark Leonardi (E. S. Townhouse, Bleckner) • Yee Kai Lim (Little Red) • Enrique Limon • Kathrine Liu (E. S. Townhouse) • Tonio Marical (A/D, Bleckner) • Todd Martin (HM/FM, J.Crew, Rifkin, Soho Loft, Metro) • Pavel Martinek (HM/FM) • Achim Marwitz (Little Red) • Lynn McCary • Marguerite McGoldrick • Greg Merryweather • Elaine Monchak (E. S. Townhouse, A/D, Bleckner, Mapplethorpe, G. V. Duplex, G. V. Townhouse) • Mark Naden • Kazem Naderi (W. V. Residence, E. S. Townhouse) • Anne Nixon (Esprit, Reservoir, Robbins, TSE) • Mariona Oliver (Little Red) • Beth O'Neill • George Perkins (Hatch, W. V. Residence, New Festival, E. S. Townhouse) • Horst Ploss • William Rockwell (Esprit) • Annette Rusin (Esprit) • Amanda Schafer • Zolaykha Sherzad • Marianne Shin (Bleckner, Mapplethorpe, Media Wall, G. V. Townhouse, Esprit, Reservoir, Robbins) • Mark Smith (W. V. Residence, New Festival, Bleckner, Mapplethorpe, G. V. Duplex, Media Wall, G. V. Townhouse, Robbins) • Tong Chol Son (Bleckner, Mapplethorpe, G. V. Duplex, G. V. Townhouse) • Gregory Stackel • Wolfgang Stöckmeier (Bleckner, G. V. Townhouse) • Tom Strub (Bleckner, G. V. Duplex, G. V. Townhouse) • Ralf Stürzebecher • Molly Sullivan • Dganit Tal-Slor • Timothy Theerman (HM/FM) • Hugo van Overbeek • Jayne Whitford (Esprit) • Calvert Wright • Bobby Young (Little Red)

(Only projects featured in this book have been included in this list.)

CONSULTANTS/ADVISERS/COLLEAGUES
1986–1997

Our work would not be achieved without the dialogue with a host of professionals, engineers, architects, and designers who have assisted us in the pursuit of architecture with the contribution of their expert advice, ideas, and experience: William Andresen • Sidney Barbanel • Wilson Bassey • James Benya • Walter Berry • Roger Blum • Ann Bobco • John Boogaerts • Joseph Bresnan • Bridget Brown • Suzanne Butterfield • Harold Campbell • Hal Crosthwaite • Taffy Dahl • Alfred D'Alessio • Ross Dalland • Neal Deputy • Fred Elsasser • Claude Engle • Lotte Eskilsson • Peter Federman • Thomas Fisher • Elizabeth Frosch • Glen Garrison • Sam Gavish • Ralph Gentile • Gerry George • Robert Gogick • Wolfgang Gruschwitz • John Gullo • James Hanskat • Kitty Hawks • Philip Johnson • Leslie Kahn • Elizabeth Kapp • Shelley Karten • Donald Kaufman • John Keenan • William Lacy • Thomas Leonidas • Barry LePatner • Bruce Lilker • Martin Marcus • Mary-Clare Mazzotta • William McDonough • Cy Mills • Dennis Milsom • Ray Moses • Kent Nash • Matt Newman • Jeffrey Osborne • Leo Parker • William Pepper • Breck Perkins • Andrew Pisani • Ivan Pollak • Glen Reinhardt • Terence Riley • Andrew Santella • Simon Sauberman • Robert Schwartz • William Schwinghammer • Edward Sider • Robert Silman • Bruce Sinder • Joseph Tortorella • Billie Tsien • Gregory Turpan • Sara Vass • Lisa Westheimer • Tod Williams • John Wood • Phil Yee • Robert Zion

BUILDERS/ARTISANS/CRAFTSPEOPLE
1986–1997

We consistently learn a great deal from the builders, craftspeople, and others who share their knowledge and their dedication to the highest quality of construction and craftsmanship. From each of them we learn something about materials, or their assembly or finish. Our work is enriched by the experience of working with them: Ilya Asanovich • Jim Battista • John Battle • Steve Bendheim • Grant Bennett • Bob Berger • Robert Bernhardt • John Beyer • Nelson Blitz • Leon Breuer • John Briggs • Tony Brown • Uwe Brueggemann • Steve Buckley • Tony Caccamo • Michael Chandler • Paul Chrystal • Chris Clark • Douglas Cohen • Bill Correa • Roger Delaney • John De Lorenzo • Tom De Lorenzo • Augusto de Oliveira • Dominic de Oliveira • Frank de Oliveira • Victor de Oliveira • Paul Deutsch • Tim Doyle • Duane Dugan • Alex Duke • Bob Ebner • Jeff Ehrlich • Dana Eldridge • Charles Flickinger • John Flynn • Todd Fouser • Greg Gannon • Tadeusz Gawel • Milton Goldworth • James Gould • Hans Gransjean • Jens Grundmann • Tom Hand • Dick Hannington • Hans Hase • Gee Heckscher • Jochem Hendricks • Andy Hoffman • Greg Hood • Catherine Hough • John Houshmond • Evan Hughes • Jodi Intermont • Isaiah Johnson • Mary Jones • Nick Jordache • Larry Kahn • Stanley Kaplan • David Kelleran • Ed Kelly • John Kern • Victor Khanin • George Kivotidis • Bob Kraus • Sam Kwan • Paul LaCour • Michael LaPenna • Steven Lamazor • Fred Larson • Joe Laurie • Gerry Lawrence • Jeremy Lebensohn • John Leoung • Pavel Lerman • Ron Lessard • Paul Lindo • Sherrill Mass • Michael McFadden • Steve McMahon • Wesley Medeiros • Henry Mendler • Joseph Mendler • Calvin Mooney • Nate Morton • Paul Nippes • John F. Noons • Breck Perkins • Rich Pinto • Barbara Piscuskas • Kathryn Piscuskas • Richard Piscuskas • Stephen Piscuskas • Juan Puntes • Peter Read • Edgar Renovales • Jon Rickard • Karl-Hans Riehm • Willi Riehm • Danielle Robbiani • Tom Robinson • Robert Rudd • Bill Russell • Frederick Sandor • David Schlakett • Katrin Schnabl • Jeffrey Shier • Dan Silberman • Stanley Snyder • David Spector • Ted Thirlby • Steve Treslow • Steve Tringale • Jimmy Tuohy • Larry Turk • John Ulewitz • Len Wersan • Ted Weuker • John Williams • Eric Winslow • David Wong • James Wong • Steven Wray • Dan Wreck • Ken Wright • B. Wurtz • Edward Youkilis • Robert Younger • Benny Zale

BIBLIOGRAPHY

Wissinger, Joanna. "Separate but Equal." *Progressive Architecture*, Sept. 1985, 120–21.

Brozen, Kenneth. "The Ten Most." *Interiors*, Dec. 1985, 140–45, 182.

1100 Architect: Selected Work. Essay by Peter Cook. Catalog. Frankfurt: Z.B. Galerie, 1986.

MacNair, Andrew. "40 under 40." *Interiors*, Sept. 1986, 169.

Janjigian, Robert, with, Laura J. Haney. *High Touch: The New Materialism in Design.* New York: E. P. Dutton, 1987, 70–71.

Plumb, Barbara. "The Artists' Artist." *Vogue,* June 1987, 122.

Giovannini, Joseph. "Undesign: Out with Aggressive Decor." *New York Times,* June 1988.

Gandee, Charles. "The Young Contenders: The Next Generation of New York Architects." *House and Garden,* Aug. 1988, 96–99.

Stanfill, Francesca. "The Eyes of Kitty Hawks." *Vogue,* Aug. 1988, 372–77, 388.

Wissinger, Joanna. "P/A Profile: 1100 Architect." *Progressive Architecture,* Sept. 1988, 92–99.

Klotz, Heinrich, with Luminita Sabua, eds., *New York Architecture 1970–1990.* Frankfurt: Deutsches Architektur Museum, 1989, 114–17.

Stephens, Suzanne. "Currents." *New York Times,* Feb. 22, 1990.

Pittel, Christine. "Prototypalism." *7 Days,* Apr. 1990, 27.

A.F.C. "Building Reputations." *Vanity Fair,* June 1990.

"Primary Spaces." *House and Garden,* July 1991.

Fisher, Thomas. "Mapplethorpe and Mies." *Progressive Architecture,* Sept. 1991, 124–27.

MacIsaac, Heather Smith. "Light Motifs." *House and Garden,* Oct. 1991, 174–81, 212.

White, Constance C. R. "The New Esprit Decor." *Women's Wear Daily,* Oct. 23, 1991, 18.

Behlen, Caroline. "Robert Mapplethorpe Foundation." *Bauwelt,* Feb. 1992, 280–81.

White, Constance C. R. "Tompkins Gets Her Line." *Women's Wear Daily,* Mar. 2, 1992.

Fisher, Thomas. "The Free Plan Idea." *Progressive Architecture,* Sept. 1992, 66–71.

Cheever, Susan. "Donald Sultan's Soho Evolution." *Architectural Digest,* Sept. 1993, 116–21.

Vigano, Vanessa. "Abitare Nel Deposito." *Lighting Design & Technoshow,* Dec. 1993, 28–31.

Conran, Terence. *The Essential House Book.* London: Conran Octopus, 1994.

Henderson, Justin. "Esprit's New Spirit." *Interiors,* Jan. 1994, 90–91.

Stephens, Suzanne. "Spotlight: 1100 Architect." *Oculus,* Feb. 1994, 8–9.

Iovine, Julie V. "Lux Boheme." *New York Times*, Feb. 1994, 58–63.

Viladas, Pilar. "Architecture: 1100 Architect." *Architectural Digest*, July 1994, 44, 48, 50.

Abram, Joseph. "Réalisme et Rationalité." *FACES Journal D'Architectures,* fall 1994, 31.

Goodman, Wendy. "Landmark of Luxury." *Harper's Bazaar,* Feb. 1995, 127–28.

Vass, Sara. "Buy Design." *The Zine,* Feb. 1995, 43–45.

Vigano, Vanessa. "Lo Spirito D'Esprit." *Lighting Design & Technoshow,* Feb. 1995.

"An Elegant Store for Cashmere." *Progressive Architecture,* Mar. 1995, 27.

"Anziehendes Projekt." *Männer Vogue,* June 1995, 112–13.

Abercrombie, Stanley. "1100 Architect." *Interior Design,* Sept. 1995, 164–67.

"The AD 100 Designers and Architects." *Architectural Digest*, Sept. 1995, 54.

Weber, Annette. "Zarte Versuchung." *Elle Germany,* Sept. 1995, 190.

Viladas, Pilar. "Traditional Modernism: Kitty Hawks' New York Country House." *Architectural Digest,* Oct. 1995, 194–203.

Madden, Chris Casson. *Bathrooms.* New York: Clarkson Potter, 1996.

Hayward, Brooke. "Love in Tune." *Town and Country,* June 1996, 122–29, 172.

Wedekind, Beate. *New York Interiors.* Ed. Anjelika Taschen. New York: Taschen, 1997, 200–209.

Kuczynski, Alex. "Minimalist Chic Shrinks the Big City." *New York Observer,* Jan. 29, 1997, 1, 19.

"TSE: 1100 Architect." *Shoten Kenchiku,* Mar. 1997, 209.

Drewes, Frank F. "Light Lenses." *Licht & Architektur* 18 (1997): 8.

Viladas, Pilar. "Uptown Downtown." *New York Times Magazine,* June 29, 1997, 46–51.

PHOTOGRAPHY CREDITS

All photography by Michael Moran with the exception
of the following (numbers refer to page numbers):

Rolf Abraham: 18, 140, 142, 144, 147

Oberto Gili: 118

Jens Grundman: 23, 24, 25, 26, 27

Joachim Hopp: 10, 11, 184, 185, 186, 187, 188, 189

Achim Marwitz: 56

Juergen Riehm: 50, 121, 123

Sharon Risedorph: 158, 159, 160, 161, 162, 163

Joseph White: 165, 167

Paul Warchol: 134, 137, 138